Advance Praise for

Street Kids and Streetscapes:
Panhandling, Politics, and Prophecies

"Marjorie Mayers declares that from her work with 'street kids' her eyes were opened in new ways. The passion in her work must be a by product of this new vision. My reading of her book offers me critical insight into my own life as viewed through the lives of the marginalized others. This time those others—street kids—look like my own children. I've always thought that there is much to be learned from our children, and Marjorie Mayers articulates this wisdom. This is an important work for educators and for parents."

Alan Block, Professor of Education,
University of Wisconsin-Stout

"This is one of those books that I'm always a wee bit afraid to read, because, right from the start, I know that the life I've lived and the assumptions I've all-too-easily made, are going to be in for a long, tough ride. As Gadamer once whispered in my ear, all experience worthy of the name involves suffering. Read this. It's worth it."

David Jardine, Professor of Education,
University of Calgary

"Marjorie Mayers has not only written a powerful and moving account of what it means to be a street kid, she has also provided us with a stellar example of how to take an interpretive approach to inquiry. This is no smoothed account, but a vivid, heart-wrenching portrayal of the struggle to be recognized, both for the researcher and her participants. The people that live in this document show us what it means to care about something deeply enough to pay loving attention to it."

Jim Field, Professor of Education,
University of Calgary

Ayerø

Street Kids
& Streetscapes

Studies in the
Postmodern Theory of Education

Joe L. Kincheloe and Shirley R. Steinberg
General Editors

Vol. 181

PETER LANG
New York • Washington, D.C./Baltimore • Bern
Frankfurt am Main • Berlin • Brussels • Vienna • Oxford

Marjorie Mayers

Street Kids
& Streetscapes

Panhandling, Politics,
& Prophecies

PETER LANG
New York • Washington, D.C./Baltimore • Bern
Frankfurt am Main • Berlin • Brussels • Vienna • Oxford

Library of Congress Cataloging-in-Publication Data

Mayers, Marjorie.
Street kids and streetscapes: panhandling, politics,
and prophecies / Marjorie Mayers.
p. cm. – (Counterpoints; vol. 181)
Includes bibliographical references.
1. Street children–United States. 2. Homeless youth–United States.
3. Homelessness–Government policy–United States. 4. Homelessness–
Moral and ethical aspects–United States. I. Title.
II. Counterpoints (New York, N.Y.); vol. 181.
HV875.55 .M38   362.76'0973–dc21   00-062973
ISBN 0-8204-5218-1
ISSN 1058-1634

Die Deutsche Bibliothek-CIP-Einheitsaufnahme

Mayers, Marjorie:
Street kids and streetscapes: panhandling, politics,
and prophecies / Marjorie Mayers.
–New York; Washington, D.C./Baltimore; Bern;
Frankfurt am Main; Berlin; Brussels; Vienna; Oxford: Lang.
(Counterpoints; Vol. 181)
ISBN 0-8204-5218-1

Front and back cover photos taken by Debra Schuler-Murray

The paper in this book meets the guidelines for permanence and durability
of the Committee on Production Guidelines for Book Longevity
of the Council of Library Resources.

© 2001 Peter Lang Publishing, Inc., New York

Printed in the United States of America

For those who shared their stories with me
and for those still waiting to be heard.

Table of Contents

Acknowledgments

I don't know where to begin. I'm not sure how, in the course of one page or so, I can acknowledge the people who have helped me along the way, who have contributed to the fruition of this book. This journey has been difficult and, at times, more than I thought I could bear. There have been individuals beside me who have helped me persevere, people who coaxed and cajoled me, people who reminded me when I had forgotten why this work is important to me and also why this work is important beyond me. I could never name everyone who has made a difference, but rest assured that many people have.

I am deeply indebted to two kindred souls who travel with me in my journeys and never leave me to walk difficult paths on my own. To Ginny Stroeher, who always lent an attentive ear and was consistently available to listen to me read portions of this manuscript over the phone, thank you for being a constant source of support, wisdom, thoughtful guidance, friendship, laughter, and love. To Tom Pirosok, without whom this book would never have come into being, thank you for sharing alternative visions of the world with me and for never losing hope for a more peaceful existence even when I'm certain that its achievement is impossible. Thank you for your tireless, detailed editing expertise, for your insightful and engaging criticism, for endlessly loving and supporting me, and, generally, for being my hero.

I can't say enough about how I am eternally grateful to my fantastic parents, Eunice and Bobby Mayers, for supporting me throughout these years, for teaching me about looking after the world, and for instilling in me the values of learning, justice, and action. Without them, this work would not have been possible.

Many thanks also go to David Jardine, for offering kind words and pearls of wisdom exactly at the right moments. And to Jim Field, for whom I have developed a deep love and respect and to whom I owe a great debt of gratitude for helping me with this manuscript right from the word go.

And certainly not least, but indeed last, to my editors and soul-friends, Shirley Steinberg and Joe Kincheloe, a gargantuan thank you for finding me, for trusting me, and for giving me the opportunity to share this learning with others.

It is not incumbent on [us] to finish the task —
neither are [we] free to desist from it

Ancient Kabbalistic saying about the task
of repairing the world, Pirke Avot 2:16

Chapter One

An Invitation for Reading

Before you there is a document
   carefully and thoughtfully composed.
Before you there are voices,
   waiting in the pages, lurking in the margins.

Inside you there are stories
There are memories of your coming to be

These pages are like wandering souls—Voices emerging
   who also have tales, stories of their lives,
         memories of their coming to be
               This is their telling and mine…and yours.

Let these accounts mingle with yours.
   Let deafness hear anew. Let the words echo and linger…
         thoughts in a flicker gone and back once more.
   Let them dangle and resonate in the jigsaw of our understandings

Let these stories terrify you, anger you, sadden you, shake you.
   Let them not touch you—leave them, take them, believe them, don't.

They are offered in kindness, in criticism, in hope.
   They are pleas and apologies, cries and creations and they are angry and
        glad—desperate and free.

This is my offering,
   it is the communion of an understanding and a possibility for hope.
   It is a manifestation of compassion, of redress, of guilt and love and hate.
       I offer it to ears and eyes,
hearts and minds,
   intellect and emotion,
       I offer it to you.

Street kids are the focus of this book. I will not say why yet, or how, or what aspect of street kids has captured me throughout this work because I must first settle, for you and me, that although street kids are central to the topic at hand, this inquiry itself has grown, and evolved, and changed. I can tell you, however, that it is them who have seized me, who have presented themselves in the world as I experience it as people to encounter, to engage, to explore, to learn from, to let teach me, to heal me, to show me. Gadamer (1977) says that "we are possessed by something and precisely by means of it we are opened up for the new, the different, the true" (9). And so it is true of this work. Street kids possess me and beckon my coming to understand something new about them, and about me, and, reluctant as you may be, also about you. Through the traces and trails of this journey, you will come to know that although this book is about street kids, it is also about more than that. This book is as much about the process of doing hermeneutic work, as much about academic hegemony, and as much about the larger sociopolitical context in which street kids are situated as it is about anything else. The intentions of this book are manifold, but they converge in the intent of illuminating something new, different, and compelling about street kids and our lives with them.

In order that I can make an attempt to bring expression to what I have learned and experienced about street kids and about the world in which we live, I must first invite you to explore my worldview as it relates to the nature and importance of interpretive inquiry. I must first ask you to engage this text in a way that will free you from the constraints that bind scholarly inquiry into a narrow set of acceptable procedural rules and evidentiary standards in the hope of creating a space for an unencumbered understanding about street kids and allowing a newness about the topic to emerge.

"[T]he real power of hermeneutical consciousness is our ability to see what is questionable" (Gadamer, 1977, 13), and so it has been my task to look anew at all that complicates and confounds an understanding of street kids. The central tenet of this kind of inquiry is to make meaning and in some way to impart that meaning in a pedagogic and transformative way (Gallagher, 1992; Smith, 1994). It is not about separating and holding in abeyance our experiences in life; on the contrary, it is precisely because of our history that we seek to bring to bear what might be otherwise lurking quietly behind the scenes. It is not about reproducing the world so that there is a finite, obdurate, static truth that can be measured against some other truth, but rather it is about engaging in the dialectic and multilayered conversation that is continually in flux, changing, evolving, and shifting. It is about a kind of personal acuity that enlists us to take up life and all that is mingled in living's complexities despite our desires for certainty and predictability. For me, this has meant that this work has been profoundly pedagogical in terms of learning about the conditions and particularities of street kids' lives and the connections they have to my life and to all of our lives. It has involved continuous, multifaceted dialogues between myself and a host of conversants, conversants with whom you will become acquainted throughout this text. For example, in Chapter Two, I explore how my situatedness in the landscape of the street kid topic emerged and how it led me to take on the exploration of kids' lives on the street. I explain how engaging the literature on street kids to glean a better understanding of what academia could offer on the subject led me to approach this inquiry in a particular way, and so on.[1]

Throughout this work you will become familiar with the multiple conversations simultaneously converging on the topic of street kids, conversations that include myself, street kids, the literature, and my own reflections. This process has enabled me to understand something about street kids, about myself, and about the world in which we live that I did not understand in the same way before. It is this understanding that I will share in the following chapters and pages. For street kids, I imagine that this process has meant an opportunity to interpret their lives and experiences in order to teach me something about them and their lives on the street. It has meant that through our conversations they have expressed the connections and meanings they have come to understand about themselves and their world with the goal of telling me something about the conditions of their lives. Understanding through interpretation is the hermeneutic quest and "good interpretation shows the connection between experience and expression" (Smith, 1994, 107). This is what I hope to do here. It is the goal of my efforts and it is the labor of this book to show you,

---

[1] For a more traditional review of the literature, please see Appendix I: Re-reading Street Kids

to engage you, and to help you understand. The hermeneutic mandate is an impressive one, but it also seems to be an articulation of the most natural form of communication, of conversation, of questioning, and of living. It is, after all, a philosophy of living, not a prescription for inquiry. But despite hermeneutics' encompassing characteristics, it can nevertheless be situated within a research landscape and can offer invaluable insights into why, how, and in what manner one might take up the complexities of a question and, ultimately, the messiness of an answer.

Phenomenologically speaking, being seized by a topic, as I have been, is already admitting that we are interpretive beings and that the intention with which we attend to something speaks to our natural inclinations to attend in the first place (Smith, 1994). This can be traced to Husserl's notion of intentionality (we are always conscious of a something) and to the phenomenologist's commitment to the lifeworld[2] (Caputo, 1987; Smith, 1994). And so, the lifeworld inhabited by street kids is central to what we are discussing here. Partly because of my intention to investigate the lived experiences of street kids, partly because street kids had an opportunity to talk about their lives and to discuss their lived experiences, and partly because I am hoping to engage you in this discussion, a dialogic conversation has begun. From this place of experience and expression, I will lead you, and beckon you, and show you.

Gadamer (1995) suggests that this intermingling of our knowing and understanding, of our beliefs and perspectives, is a fusion of horizons where we reach in for the common ground between us, using language, history, and conversation to mediate our communication. This is done in the spirit of understanding and renovation. In this case, the intention is to get closer to the lives of street kids and to understand those life stories for all the things that they may tell us, things we might be ready for as well as things that might surprise us. It is to follow the threads of conversations that lead to various places and diverse understandings. There is no unbiased

---

[2] Husserl's contribution to this discussion rests primarily in his disavowing metaphysics as the central concern for philosophy and in refocusing philosophical questions away from ontology and toward the world as it is experienced. However, Husserl's reductions and beliefs in universal essences are not consistent with a hermeneutic or interpretive standpoint. For a brief explication of phenomenology's contribution to the development of philosophical hermeneutics, see Gallagher (1992); Smith (1994).

position from whence to offer up a value-free assessment, to extricate information from its context. We always begin from a perspective and carry with us our history, language, purposes, and convictions. In other words, there is no way of getting behind perspective—there is no place of pristine tabula rasa from which to depart. The point of departure is always referential and prejudiced, relational and prejudged in terms of one's history and all that is invoked by one's tradition. And that is true of me, of the kids, and of you.

But this admission need not frighten us, for it is a path of honesty and hope. Tradition or perspective need not translate into the narcissist's ego fantasy, luring us into a world that is separate and cloistered from anything else we might know or understand. It is rather about the interplay between experience and understanding, between situating what is new in relation to what we may already surmise and where our understanding may already be. It is, in the end, a practical approach to dialogue, dialectic, and discovery (Dewey, 1916; Gadamer, 1995; Gallagher, 1992). And herein lies the point of this book. It is to admit that there are multiple perspectives about street kids and to cogently offer one here. It is to connect the familiar to the unfamiliar and to find our way through the tensions of both. It is to present a case for an interpretation of the lived experiences of street kids and what that potentially means to me, to you, and to our understanding of the phenomenon. And so, despite the misunderstanding that interpretation is about the self, the ego, and the solipsistic space of the interpreter, good interpretation is certainly not. Hermeneutical interpretation can never be merely about the reconstruction of the world as it is, or as the narcissist sees it, but rather is always an open approach to questioning and understanding the meanings that erupt in the geographies that we are exploring. It is about understanding ourselves by way of understanding others, and I will therefore attempt to show you the manifold ways that these connections encounter the topic.

Gadamer (1995) suggests that history and language act as both constraints and liberators in terms of our own understandings. This does not mean that once you have understood yourself you are all of a sudden able to see things as they actually are—definitively, finally—but rather that constant reflection is a necessary component of exploration that has as its core the careful scrutiny of ourselves, of others, and of the world as it presents itself beyond what we may be prepared for. Admitting in advance that I have a perspective is not a justification for saying anything at all about street kids. In the first place, my perspective is a dynamic energy of thoughts, reflections, learning, questioning, feeling, and assessing. I am continually muddling through to make meaning of the things that are presented to me as well as the things that I seek out. Gadamer (1995) suggests that this is precisely how I may be able to maintain my openness about the topic. And so this book is an invitation for me to show you how my history, how my language, and how my perspective open me to the possibilities of interpretation, possibilities that erupt in the generative engagement and search for meaning with the topic at hand (Jardine, 1992). "History is only present to us in light of our futurity" (Gadamer, 1977, 9). And so it is that hermeneutics recognizes the centrality of the tradition from whence one speaks, set among and in between the fluid motion of the world. Indeed, it is precisely because of my history, my beliefs, and my ideas that I have arrived at this point of asking questions about street kids.

Understanding and interpretation come from a tension that lives in between what is familiar to us and what is unfamiliar. This means that coming to this inquiry has been based on some familiar understanding of what the lived experiences of street kids might be. But the conversation doesn't end because of my familiarity with the topic. In other words, I am not trying to fit what I find out into what I already know. Hermeneuts contend that what is familiar to us opens up the topic precisely because it presents itself as unfamiliar. As an example, making sense of the literature that I read on street kids as part of my becoming familiar with the topic was influenced both by my historical experience of previously working with street kids and from the projection of future understandings based on questions that I asked the literature to answer. Information I gleaned from reading the literature led me further to ask new questions about street kids, stemming from both my experience working with street kids as well as from having a familiarity with the literature. And so it goes that hermeneutics is pushed and propelled by the questions that we ask and the understandings that throw into question what we thought we already understood. This is where interpretation resides, oscillating amid what we understand and what we don't, what is familiar to us and what is not. Gallagher (1992) says that "[i]nterpretation is an attempt to responsibly bridge these two demands [i.e., what is familiar and what is unfamiliar], to resolve or in some way to deal with the tension between them" (150). To that end, this inquiry prompted me to ask questions of street kids, to vacillate between what I already understood and what was still foreign to me, and to take up the tensions that arise in the discourses of the street for kids.

As I've noted, it is my task to artfully bring to bear in expression what has been experienced, and, to that end, you also play a part. In as much as text engages a reader and from that engagement a relationship is born, the dialectics of understanding, communication, questions, and thoughts are initiated between us. That is, the text is restored to a living communication when it is taken up, when it is read, when it is interpreted (Ricoeur, 1981). I offer this text as a pedagogic encounter for all of us. I hope that the relationship that you will have with this text, and that I have had with this text over many years and months, will be an opportunity for learning. We are engaged, you and me, and our lives will never be the same because we are the accumulations of our experiences and are ever-changing beings because of our experiences. Above and beyond what we will or want, the lifeworld calls us and we are intertwined in it. We are called, as it were, to pay careful attention. It is to that existential state that hermeneutics invites us. And it is to that flux of dynamics between all that makes this book what it is that I invite you.

So how might we take up that invitation? How might we judge an interpretation? What counts as evidence for the interpretation that I will offer here? In much of Gadamer's *Truth and Method* (1995), he refutes scientific claims to truth and authority. He battles with positivist conceptions of objectivity and reason and, in their stead, offers an alternative view of epistemology. But if not in a static measure for our claiming to know something, then how can we determine the extent to which understanding has occurred? Or, how can we be certain that an adequate interpretation has been rendered? These are the questions that I must take up so that you may read this book armed with the hermeneutic measures used to judge the value of the evidence offered.

> [G]ood interpretation is a creative act on the side of sharpening identity within the play of differences—and we thereby give voice to and show

features of our lives ordinarily suppressed under the weight of the dominant economic, political, and pedagogical fundamentalisms of the time. (Smith, 1994, 123)

To enable insights to emerge that begin to answer the questions of what hermeneutics is concerned with and ultimately what good interpretation leads to, I will take up three central tenets of philosophical hermeneutics and provide brief examples of how these tenets relate to the lived experiences of street kids. Questions, understanding, and the hermeneutic circle suggest the parameters (or the boundlessness) of how we might engage a topic and what we might do once we are in the middle of it. These components are not clearly delineative, and, thus, their explication does not lend itself to linear articulation. They need to be understood as a complex of interdependent ideas that reflect the possibilities that interpretive inquiry offers. Questions and the complexity of openness, issues around understanding and the fertility of how understanding comes to be, and the hermeneutic circle, understood as the interpretive inertia which continually churns and alters questions and understandings, will enable us to proceed in taking up the complexities of street kids' lives. Hermeneutics is about finding your way, and likewise, in finding mine, I must first enjoin with you. As Gadamer (1995) states: "The first condition of the art of conversation is ensuring the other person is with us" (367).

Questions

Questions and openness are central to the hermeneutical endeavor. As Gadamer (1995) contends, "the question is the path to knowledge" (363). For me, this has meant a program of research by question as opposed to only by method. In terms of this research, my questions began years ago when I worked with street kids and formally continued during my surveying of the literature and formulation of questions to ask street kids for this inquiry. But, as the hermeneutic endeavor commands, questions beget questions, and so it is true of what transpired for me once engaged with street kids. Although the questions that I asked street kids were fairly consistent (i.e., "What is it like being a street kid?" or "Tell me your story"), the replies which were offered led me to ask questions beyond what I was asking the kids. These questions included political and social questions about Western culture and North American values, questions about poverty and service delivery, questions about social strata, and so on. Interpretive scholars understand that taking up a topic involves following the trails forged by the substantive qualities imbedded in the topic and by the questions which are raised in the pursuit of its understanding (see, for example, Denzin, 1997; Gadamer, 1977, 1995; Gallagher, 1992; Jardine, 1990, 1992; Smith, 1994). Each question directs us toward or away from understanding, but questions always drive what we uncover, what we wonder about, what we admit we do not know. "A question places what is questioned in a particular perspective. When a question arises, it breaks open the being of the object as it were" (Gadamer, 1995, 362). Therefore, in the act of inquiry, we must situate our questions within the domains of our own understandings so that they can be laid open to possibilities. The hermeneutical understanding of the foregrounded question is that which stems forth from a position, that which is exposed to whatever hinders or helps propel the question beyond itself. "The important thing is to be aware of one's own bias, so that the text can present itself in all its otherness and thus assert its own truth against one's own fore-meaning" (Gadamer, 1995, 269). After all, we are ultimately concerned with understanding and meaning, and, therefore, the extent to which a question reveals the possibilities of what might be will determine to some extent the value of the question itself.

And so in the trajectory of my work I've been compelled by some questions while quieting and laying others aside. Jardine (1992) notes that knowing in advance which threads to follow and which to lay aside is indeterminable until such time as the leads lead nowhere. Perhaps this is one of the aspects of hermeneutics which we can perceive and judge, which can help us conclude whether or not an adequate interpretation has been rendered. Are our questions evoking more questions? Are they leading us somewhere else—somewhere beyond the boundaries of what we already know, or think, or feel?

Questioning "is more a passion than an action. A question presses itself on us, we can no longer avoid it and persist in our accustomed opinion" (Gadamer, 1995, 366), and so our ideas and beliefs change, our directions turn, and our understandings deepen. For example: As a result of reading the literature for what it could tell me about street kids, I was struck by the pervasive use of quantitative methodologies. Ultimately, I thought, these research designs produce certain kinds of data—data that I believed to be devoid of street kids' lived experiences. There were a myriad of questions that arose for me as I read through that body of literature. This culminated in my decision to ask the kids what being a street kid is like. This question seemed to open up the possibilities for answers and understandings that I could not imagine in advance. It left room for the familiar to emerge as unfamiliar. At the same time, however, there were questions that I believed would surface through my conversations with street kids that didn't really surface. Although I was interested in investigating patriarchy and pecking order on the street, it was not an issue that arose or, should I say, that arose in a way that led me to investigate it further. This is an instance where I chose to leave a question unanswered, ununderstood, and unattended to.

Gleaning interpretive inquiry's emphasis on questioning and openness, and accepting that one's fore-understanding is both an impediment and opportunity to understanding (i.e., recognizing that one speaks out of a tradition and that one's inquiry is bound up in the tension between the familiar and the unfamiliar), we get a little closer to what understanding might be and how understanding comprises both conversation and interpretation. Gallagher (1992) suggests that our fore-understanding is "...continually being modified by experience; it can be radically altered and corrected as it proceeds to understanding" (69). Understanding is conceived as a fluid process, ceaselessly mediated by a constant revisioning of what has been previously understood. The interplay between what is new and what seems familiar is where the interpretive conversation is located. Hermeneutics is centered in "open[ing] up something that seemed 'over and done with'" (Jardine, 1992, 55). The tension between the known and the needing to be known rests in the conversing and languaging that we do to figure out what is at play.

Language

Language, as Gadamer (1995) emphasizes, is central to the way understanding is experienced. In the first place, a conversation is always a conversation about something, and, in the second place, a conversation is dialectically engaged by languaging about that something. Hermeneutics prescribes that we enter into multiple dialogues at multiple levels. Here, for example, I am both conversing with the texts that explicate the interpretive nature of conversation, dialectic, and dialogue, and simultaneously, I am conversing with you and with this text. Invested in these conversations, there is an impetus to arrive at some shared meaning, some shared conception of what this text is revealing about hermeneutic understanding and conversation. Similarly, in the course of this book, I have initiated multiple conversations with multiple conversants. As previously mentioned, these conversants have been talking with me about street life for kids. I have grappled and swayed in the decisions that direct which questions persist in asking for reconciliation and which understandings I might follow and explore. I am continually engaged in a dialogic conversation with myself, with others, with literature, with participants, with society, and with the world. To that end, the entire interpretive turn is about conversation and renovation. To signify the multivocality imbedded in this topic and, therefore, in this text, and as a way of representing the myriad conversations that happen all at once, I have tried to preserve the various voices that inform and mediate the complexity of coming to any kind of understanding about street kids. Perhaps we might say that understanding is temporarily achieved when something new emerges about a topic which leads us to someplace else. In this case, perhaps we might posit that understanding "of the particular case leads us to understand the universal" (Gallagher, 1992, 342), all the while knowing that understanding and learning are never complete or final.

The Hermeneutic Circle

One way of conceiving of this convergence of voice and conversation, of understanding and reflection in interpretive inquiry, is to invoke the hermeneutic circle. The hermeneutic circle is interpretive inquiry's way of letting meaning and understanding unfold through the constant renewal of questions and conversation. This process is fluid. It has movement like the gentle (or maybe not so gentle) ebb and flow of the ocean's tide. The hermeneutic circle refers to the interplay between parts and wholes where "...the meaning of the part is only understood within the context of the whole, but the whole is never given unless through an understanding of the parts. Understanding therefore requires a circular movement from parts to whole and from whole to parts" (Schleirermacher, cited in Gallagher, 1992, 59).

And so this process of questioning and understanding, reflecting and questioning again, reveals the unending reciprocity between thinking, feeling, experiencing, and interpretation. The hermeneutic circle, therefore, implies a temporality, a contextual referent or chronological stream of turnings and twistings which contiguously evolve in relation to a topic. As a result of each experience which beckons our intention and calls our attention to it, we accumulate a knowing that propels us into the future, all the while incorporating our understandings of the past. With street kids, this has meant a continuous process of reflection on what it means to live as a street kid. Informed partly by the conversations that I have had with street kids, and partly by what strikes me anew while thinking about the topic, I am constantly cycling in questioning and understanding—reflection that repeats back on itself, always taking into account the diverse teachings the kids offered, always turning toward what emerges as unfamiliar. The process evolved and revolved, always enlarging itself to incorporate new aspects of understanding, producing more questions, leading me in deeper and in new directions. As Gadamer (1995) notes: "The art of questioning is the art of questioning even further—i.e., the art of thinking" (367).

I believe this is true of my exploration into the lived experiences of street kids. Even as I write this invitation for reading, I realize that my understandings about the topic have changed from when I first began "turning towards the phenomenon" (van Manen, 1991). For example, I originally imagined that the data I would collect would be replete with particularities about street kids' home life experiences. To my surprise, the greatest proportion of (and what had the greatest impact on me) what kids talked about had much less to do with the homes they had come from than the lives they were currently living on the street. This is demonstrative of interpretive inquiry's imbedded regenerative process. In the pursuit of bringing expression to the experienced, I will try to account for those circular turnings and twistings that make up my ever-evolving and incomplete understandings about the lives of street kids. This inertia between expected and unexpected, questions and more questions, understanding and interpretation, reveals itself as an ever-enlarging proposition increasingly open to thoughtful and provocative interpretation. As Gallagher (1992) concludes, "[t]he more movement in the circle, the larger the circle grows, embracing the expanding contexts that throw more and more light upon the parts" (59), the greater the potential for a more comprehensive interpretation to emerge. And so it is true of this inquiry. At one time I was looking to fill in some of the gaps that had been left by the literature. Currently, much more is in question and much more has been implicated in understanding the lived experiences of street kids.

Hermeneutics Closer to the Street

As I have stated, my approach emanated from my dissatisfaction with the unidirectional, positivist, and quantitative approaches that researchers have traditionally taken with this population. Nevertheless, the literature on street kids has defined, delineated, and dissected the various aspects of becoming a street kid. From familial background to behavior on the street, this body of research has identified a number of issues which street kids confront both before getting to the street and subsequent to living on the street. The literature provides a solid demographic, quantitative perspective of street kids, including potential antecedent factors. But my approach is obviously different. My approach emanates from my worldview, a perspective that is incongruent with the positivists' entitled fix on truth and authority. It emanates from my seeing and understanding something different about the phenomenon. It emanates from a drive away from compartmentalized understanding and a drive toward a more holistic and ecological rendering of what is at play. Its impetus is to understand what is going on for street kids with all its potential messiness. I appreciated the literature as it explicated aspects of what it might be like to be a street kid, and I understood the literature as a starting point from which I could launch my own scholarly thinking about the subject.[3]

I assessed that the meaning of being a street kid was not evident in the academic literature, largely as a result of the overwhelming use of quantitative design in the research methodology. This book is an attempt to begin to redress that literature lacuna. More than an opportunity to try a different research approach, it is about looking at street kids from a completely different perspective. For me, this was an invitation to disrupt the current propositions about street kids and to use language to effect that goal (Bonneycastle, 1996). Smith (1994) tells us that good interpretive research "problematize[s] the hegemony of dominant culture in order to engage it transformatively" (114). For me, hermeneutics, and all that it encompasses in terms of questioning, understanding, reflecting and renewing, was the natural choice to make. Interpretive work was, and is, my chosen path because it most closely embodies the philosophy according to which I live my life. It is like finding a soul mate, a companion who helps clarify the confusion, who helps figure out the complexities, and who sometimes insists that we linger in the messiness of the issues so that we are receptive and open to learning something new.

The goals I set out for this inquiry seemed simple. I wanted to investigate the lived experiences of street kids. I wanted to ask them what being a street kid is like, and what meanings they ascribe to their lives. I wanted to explore the multiple discourses of the street. I wanted to understand something new about street kids. What seemed simple those years ago seems more complicated now. Gadamer (1995) suggests that the danger of interpretive work is losing oneself in the fray of the complexity of the lifeworld, and so it is that this kind of research is deeply personal (but not private). Jardine (1992) acknowledges that there are directions and leads that arise from our research that we leave untouched and unexamined, and we must admit that we are uncertain of the places those paths would have led. Hermeneutics does not ask us to take everything up, but rather to explore what erupts for us, beyond us, and inspire of us.

---

[3] I refer here specifically to a scholarly endeavor as a way of delineating that my turning toward the topic began long before I connected with the academic literature. This will be further explicated in Chapter Two.

When I was a doctoral student, it was incumbent upon me to figure out how I was going to do this research. As I learned about research methodology and about the philosophy of science, I travelled through the worlds of a number of research approaches. I must confess now that building a research methodology was more of an "academic-process" concern than a philosophical need. For me, how I might approach this topic as a non-academic seemed natural and easy, seemed simple and uncomplicated, and so I wanted to find an academic path that would similarly resonate with how I see the world and how I come to understand things, or know things, or question things. I needed to become familiar with what adopting a certain approach might mean for me, for my participants, and for the world. I engaged the discourses of research methodology to finally (but never finally) find my place. It became clear that there could be no separation between who I am as an individual, a student, a woman, a Jew, a friend, and so on, and how I choose to take up the world. It is for those reasons that I have also come to understand that interpretive inquiry would guide me as I undertook this investigation.

Hermeneutics and Writing

Hermeneutics requires that we pay attention to language (Smith, 1994), and that we use language as the go-between in our dialogic communication. Language, according to Gadamer (1995), is everything that we can articulate; it is the culmination of our thoughts and our understandings, yet it leaves the door open for further interpretation and consideration. The centrality of language in hermeneutics has direct ramifications for writing and for writing in particular ways. Accompanied by the importance of questions and conversation, of hermeneutic circles and understandings, language undergirds all that we can bring to the interpretive engagement. Without language, we could never bring to voice what we experience, and as we have previously appreciated, good interpretation is about bringing expression to experience. Hermeneutic writing is "strong…its desire is to provoke new ways of seeing and thinking, with a deep sense of tradition, bringing about new forms of engagement and dialogue about the world we face together" (Smith, 1994, 127). And so the task of the interpretive writer is to use language and poetics, to use evocative and provocative prose to make her case, to reveal the web of connections she has cast in the confused and complicated world of understanding. The writing of the objective, disinterested observer, the value-free, unbiased, innocent reporter is unwelcome in interpretive work. Hermeneutics necessitates a deep personal involvement with the topic and the text; there is no severed position from which to report. Denzin (1997) recognizes the heavy burden placed upon interpretive researchers to defend their approach to inquiry and to "resist those who would turn ethnography into stable, realist systems of meaning" (9). Issues of authority and truth, of reflection and interpretation, are elements of this kind of writing that must be shown to be relevant and in the service of the topic. Good interpretive research is always generative and always opening up to new possibilities; therefore, interpretive writing must aid in creating those possibilities.

For me, language is a critically important aspect of the interpretive endeavor both from the perspective of understanding my data as well as from the point of view of writing this book. It is through language that I hope to communicate something new to you about street kids and about the business of our living together. It is largely through language that the kids expressed their experiences to me and shared their ideas and dreams. It is through language that I will be able to take you, to convince you, to teach you, and it is through language that I run the risk of losing you. And so, I must be vigilant and gentle, careful and powerful in the conversations that I have with you, with the texts, and with the interpretations.

The interpretive constructs discussed in this chapter have immediate significance for how I have located and situated hermeneutical concepts within this book. I have tried, in my work, to execute hermeneutical tenets in at least two ways. The first is related to the way I approached the inquiry itself (and that will become apparent by following the stories of the street), and the second is connected to the manner in which I wrote this book, as well as the way I put it together. It is the second to which I will now speak.

As you turn the pages, you will notice that there are variations in font attributes representing multiple perspectives and conversations. This is my way of maintaining the richness of the progression of thoughts and understandings without limiting discussions to linear modalities or holding in abeyance pressing and urgent musings. It is my testimony to the importance of understanding the topic from the cyclical position articulated in the hermeneutic circle and the admission that only through the parts can we come to understand the whole. Similarly, throughout the text, you will recognize that there is a narrativity, a temporality, and an evolution to what you are reading. This is my pedagogical effort to grapple with what is familiar and what may not be and to offer interpretations that bring us together in understanding something about street kids and about the world in which we live. It is the manifestation of my hermeneutic philosophy to lay a common ground upon which the questions and understandings of the topic are free to erupt and where I am free to explain or explore them. This is the way I have created conversation, the way I have tried to keep myself open to the dialogic and dialectic of understanding, interpretation, and meaning. By exposing myself and telling my stories, by reflecting on my fore-understandings and coming to know myself better, and by expressing my emerging understanding through the use of effective languaging about the topic, I hope to be able show you what I learned about kids on the street and the contexts in which they live.

Chapter Two

Coming to the Topic and Going to the Street

Positioning Myself in the Landscape of Street Kids

When I changed jobs from the sanctity of a counseling office to the frontline, working on the street with homeless kids, I learned about the realities of the marginalized. I observed the despair of the impoverished. I heard the pain in the stories youth told about their lives on the street and before. I remarked on the pervasiveness of hopelessness and helplessness among these kids. The quiet, safe, known environment of an office, juxtaposed by the frenetic, unpredictable streets of the city, illuminated the great disparity between these places and the needs of the people in them. This change of working venue marked the beginning of a personal and professional journey for me that awakened my sensibility around issues that confront street youth. I could not ignore this epiphany.

My experience with street youth dates back to over a decade ago when I worked with kids on the street through a nonprofit social service agency. As in most cities, this organization (referred to here as Youth Organization [YO]) had the corner on the social service market for children and adolescents in the region. At the outset I thought that YO was doing commendable work to help improve the living conditions for youth (both physical and psychological/emotional), but soon I started to question whether or not that was indeed the case. I was a front-line worker for homeless/runaway youth in the city's downtown and "market"[4] core and worked in several different capacities—in a drop-in center for youth (up to twenty-four years old); in the needle exchange program (free needles and HIV education/testing for IV drug users and others); and as an outreach worker primarily targeting new (or unknown) street youth and male and female prostitutes.

I wondered why YO wasn't succeeding at helping these kids change their feelings of resignation about the world and their potential to thrive and succeed in it. I learned about the harsh economic, social, and political realities that battled against these kids. And then it dawned on me—perhaps YO was part of the problem.

I spent four years on the street working with youth. I did not know then all that I have come to realize now. I recall that soon after I began working on the street, I began experiencing an uneasiness regarding the system of service that I was called upon to deliver. I remember thinking to myself, "If I feel this way about 'the system,' how must the kids feel? What messages do kids take away from the service centers that they frequent? What philosophical messages undergird the services we are offering here?" I became increasingly frustrated in my work as a result of these nagging questions. Feeling alienated from the "real" issues confronting youth and feeling disempowered to radicalize the kind of caring that was available for street kids, I began a campaign to express my concerns to my colleagues about the psychological well-being of the clients at the drop-in center. The philosophy underpinning YO's mandate was essentially benevolent; that is, we were mandated to provide a safe place where food, showers, and the necessities of daily living were dispensed. Also, we were directed to engage in counselling if the opportunity presented itself; unfortunately the counselling aspect of service was hardly the priority.

Part of the problem, as I understood it, was imbedded in the kind of service delivery program that I was involved with. At the YO drop-in

---

[4] The market area in this city is situated just north of the city's downtown business district. The area basically consists of shops and restaurants and, for most of the year, a full farmer's market. This area is the center for nightlife. It is also where the majority of social service organizations are situated (e.g., The Salvation Army, The Union Mission, drop-in centers like YO [adolescent and adult], The Shepherds of Good Hope [including a food bank], a needle exchange, Family Benefits Assistance office [welfare], and a healthy sexuality clinic).

center, youth could spend up to 12 hours a day doing virtually nothing. They were having their basic needs met in terms of shelter, food, clothing, hygiene, and so on, but there was no expectation that the kids would or should contribute to the services of which they were making use. There was even less of an expectation placed on these kids to engage in the resolution of whatever psychological trauma they had experienced in their homes or were now experiencing in their daily lives on the street. I wondered about the perceptions of these youth when they were expected to do nothing, to contribute nothing, to be nothing. I wondered how the services we were providing were helping any of these kids to build, repair, or restore their sense of themselves, their self-esteem, their sense of hope for the future. Ultimately, I interpreted YO's service to be a band-aid solution to getting kids off the street so that the merchants in the market area could feel safer about conducting their business. To my mind, these services had nothing to do with psychological health and well-being or the goal of restoring it.

As I became clearer about the issues and concerns that plagued me in my work at YO's drop-in center, I began to vocalize these concerns in terms of their philosophical and perhaps more subtle ramifications for homeless youth at team meetings. My assessment of the situation fell on deaf ears. I talked at length with colleagues, tried to articulate the problems at considerable length to my superiors, but, again, there was no response. I interpreted the lack of discourse around issues of our service delivery and the philosophical, theoretical, and practical applications thereof to be YO's desperate attempt to keep numbers of clients up so that funding for the organization would continue. That is, that YO's market share of service delivery for youth should not decrease. This, it seemed, was the goal of YO's program in the downtown core. Moreover, the best interests of the clients seemed to be the one of the last priorities on a long list of needs and services being demanded. I remarked how YO's fiscal demands were central to its survival. A societal choice, I thought. I wondered what kind of comment this was on how power structures and organizational economics determine services' priorities. To me, YO's financial reality seemed like a little microcosm of all of society's darker values, and I found myself disheartened with YO in particular and society at large. I found it hard to accept the lack of attention exercised by this organization around mental health issues. At some point, I decided that working at YO was contrary to my philosophical, therapeutic, and ethical standards, and so I decided that I would further my studies, hoping to find answers to the questions I had about service delivery and homeless youth.

I believed that there were better ways to help youth both individually and within their families, and so I chose to pursue a doctoral degree. To prepare for my dissertation, I undertook researching homeless/runaway youth and the conditions in which they live. Having had four years of employment experience working with street youth in a major city, I assumed that exploring the literature would fortify some of the practical information that I gathered as a youth worker and would easily answer the questions that I had. I was surprised to find that was not so. When I went to the literature, when I investigated what the academe had to say on the subject, I experienced the same kind of disappointment that I had had while working on the street. The sound of that economic-value-laden meta-narrative struck me, and I realized that the academe was guilty too! Guilty of what remains unclear for me, save for a common inattention to personal agency and human biography prevalent in both cases. Whatever the case, reading the literature solidified my belief that there exists a great disparity between what happens on the street and what gets reported, researched, or put into program plans. Where I expected the literature in psychology and counseling to be empathic, benevolent, and concerned with the emotional well-being of children at risk, I found the literature cold, unattached, flat, removed, and unrealistic. What I came to know as I read through the research on street kids was that the vast collection of articles and books that explored street life for youth did not at all resemble what I had lived on the streets as a youth worker.

Trying to Be Accepted: The Academe, Street Kids, and Me

I had learned lessons about the silent schisms that tripped me into crevices that lay hidden in the landscape. I twisted in painful realizations about social service institutions and felt the divide between my work experience and the literature. These tripping-holes were early indications that something more was at play vis-à-vis understanding street kids and always taught me something I didn't expect. Undertaking doctoral work was similarly a complicated journey, always throwing more and less light on what I could understand about street kids and their lives.

Every doctoral student undertakes the researching and writing of a research proposal. I was no different. My task was to illuminate the gaps evidenced in the street kid literature and present a cogent argument for the research that I was going to undertake. In general, I guess, this story is not unlike those of the multitudes of other doctoral students who do the same. But I think there is something noteworthy about my experience as I reflect on what I learned about street kids through the proposal-acceptance process, how I positioned, and was positioned by interactions with the university, and how this reflects something important about understanding street kids and marginalized voices.

After completing my research proposal, after working through the conceptual and methodological mazes that were set out before me, after thinking, and reading, and writing, I learned that the research I was proposing (i.e., going out to converse with street kids about their lives) could not be undertaken with the people with whom I intended to connect. In other words, I was not able, or rather not allowed, to interview kids under the age of eighteen. This is the age at which kids can give informed consent—it's the law—and that was that!

Hello?? What?? *Let me unpack the complexity of this without alienating anybody. Let us look at this in all its messiness without anybody feeling any blame, or shame, or both. This discussion is not about who failed, or why I didn't know about the laws governing research with minors, but why such a fact (i.e., not interviewing kids under eighteen years old) brings so much to the fore for me. It is simply a critical exploration of what, in the course of my experience, happened, and ultimately how that experience encouraged me to think about my topic differently. Having said that, let us take up what that means.*

In the first place, how arbitrary do we think the age of eighteen is? In the second place, how reasonable is it to believe that kids living on their own (i.e., without their parents) are unable to make informed-consent decisions? In the third place, how sensible is it to use the same criteria for street kids as for kids living at home? These are the questions that arose for me immediately after being told (a year into the research proposal writing process, by the way) that the university would not support such an endeavor. Needless to say, I was beside myself. Have we (adults) no respect for youth and their abilities? Oh, yes, I know, it's about protecting youth from abuses. Yes. That is certainly important and something that university and judicial institutions need to be concerned with. **But we are talking about street kids here—kids who sleep outside and fend for themselves. Surely we think that they can decide whether or not they want to talk about their lives?** *Or don't we? And in that case, perhaps we need to reflect on how we feel about youth in general. Maybe we should/could be thinking about how the difficulties in accessing marginalized populations reify the status quo and the university's distance from the lived experiences of the people and issues with whom we are wanting to connect. Maybe we could be thinking about how these rules position certain stakeholders as the arbiters of knowledge and information, the gatekeepers of whom and how you can engage in any inquiry, and how academia has become an accomplice of this hierarchy. These are the suspicions that arose and are questions that I cannot settle here. I don't imagine that I will be able to settle them anywhere, but they do beckon consideration, and that, at least, I can give them. I do understand the intent of these ethical and legal positions to be in the best interest of potential participants, but are they?*

My next step was to speak with my supervisory committee about the dilemma with which I was confronted. I was determined to get permission for this research despite the apparent illegality of it. I was deeply concerned that my work would not have integrity if I consented to either only interviewing kids over eighteen years old or pursuing the consent of parents for those under eighteen.

Basically, between my conversations with a number of professional and personal contacts and my hysteria about the focus and integrity of my work, I had decided that I could not abide asking street kids' parents whether or not their kids could participate in my study. I didn't think that it made any sense; it exhibited a lack of respect for the individuals with whom I was going to converse, and was so "adult-centered" I could hardly stand it. I deliberated about my next move—carefully trying to negotiate through the murky academic waters while being ever conscious of potential political repercussions and the need for "academic correctness."

We convened a meeting to discuss the matter. In my best interest, and in the spirit of wanting me to proceed in my graduate studies, my committee was split on the matter: Two believed interviewing only eighteen-year-olds would be fine; the other member thought that getting the research done was the most important thing, and it didn't really matter how that came to fruition. Against every fiber of my being, I agreed to interview only eighteen-year-olds.

What's the big deal? Who cares? The important thing is that I get myself on the street interviewing kids. These are the things I was hearing—get moving, keep going, this is not the fight to fight.

But after a weekend of reflection and sadness, I changed my mind. I couldn't do it and to that effect decided to engage the university's legal counsel to rule on the matter. This predicament didn't make sense to me, and I needed to be able to present a case such that this anomaly could become light in all the surrounding darkness. I met with my supervisor and informed her of my change of heart, and we proceeded to contact the university lawyer.

I needed to be able to present a case that would explicate the mitigating circumstances around informed consent with minors and to disentangle ethical versus legal arguments. It seemed to me that the university was mostly concerned about liability issues rather than ethical concerns of misconduct or potential harm to the study participants. I needed to find evidence that could support my position and could bring the voice of a marginalized position to bear on the subject. I began asking the relevant literature to answer these questions in order to understand the breadth of the issues.

As these burdens became more pressing, it dawned on me that I was being positioned as an outsider or some kind of troublemaker, or maybe I was positioning myself in that way. Nobody said anything nasty or treated me badly, but I began to feel, more acutely, how the dominant ideologies of research and academia were rubbing uncomfortably up with the needs of this topic and the needs of this research (not to mention my own needs). I interpreted this discomfort to be about dominant belief structures clashing with attempts to interrupt those structures—attempts to break away from the givens, attempts to question the powerbrokers to answer for their dominance. In a conversation long after this event occurred, someone suggested to me that the complexity of this experience was not only about me and the university, but rather represented the messiness of the topic (D.

Jardine, personal communication, May 1998). In the process of understanding experience as text (Ricoeur, 1981), in exploring the hermeneutic relationship between myself and everything around me, I imagined that perhaps I was feeling like the street kid of the university. I saw myself as she who bucks the system and wants it to respond, she who sits (or wants to sit) outside the dominant ideology reified in the status quo and wants it to change, all the while feeling the opposing resistance of institutional "smooth-running." I wanted entrance into the fray to give voice to alternative possibilities and to reaffirm why it is that we engage in research at all. For me, this WAS the fight to fight because it was about integrity—not only my own, but also the university's.

In preparation for my meeting with the university lawyer, I researched relevant literature pertaining to informed consent.[5] The search was limited, but I was able to connect with a few informants who were able to direct me. Finally, I met with the lawyer and presented my case. Armed with literature and case history, armed with legalese and conviction, I succeeded in demonstrating how the laws governing informed consent, as they relate to street kids, are inadequate to meet the needs of the population and are, in fact, inapplicable. Furthermore, I convinced the lawyer that the liability concern would be moot since I was only asking participants for pseudonyms, and there would be no way to trace the identities of participants. In terms of ethics, I suggested to the lawyer that she trust me to make professionally sound decisions about whether or not a kid could understand the nature and scope of the study sufficiently to make an informed decision about participation. She said she would think about it and would write a memo with her decision. She agreed and indicated that the work should go ahead believing the laws did not adequately include street kids and that special considerations needed to be in place so that I could continue with my research project.

Halleluyah! I had the university's blessing to go ahead. I felt exonerated—like a weight had been lifted from my shoulders and a new lease on my research's life was granted. I was thrilled about the decision

---

[5] For further information on informed consent and minors, please see: Crowhurst & Dobson (1993); Domestic Relations Act (1980); Hesson, Bakal, & Dobson (1993); Jackman Cram & Dobson (1993); University of Calgary (1996).

and was proud of my perseverance—not so much because it says anything about me, but because I knew that I was going to be able to connect with kids in a manner that I believed to be respectful of their experience and knowledge. I was going to be able to respect kids in the way that I feel they deserve, and ultimately my work was going to benefit from my convictions.

Getting Ready for the Street:
A Funny Thing Happened on the Way to My Research

I think we can agree that there is a common unhappiness that we feel when thinking about the underclass, especially when it comes to kids. We probably all believe that the very existence of street kids is deplorable and a sad comment on these poor kids' unfortunate lives. Maybe we will venture to comment on lack of parenting, hard luck, or rely on the "bad seed" explanation to illuminate our understanding of such a phenomenon. We shake our heads from side to side, horrified at the stories we hear about their lives, about their experiences before and after making their way to the street, about who they have become and who they wanted to be: Generally, these accounts are distasteful to our moral sensibilities. We have, as a collective, agreed that the disenfranchised need our help, and so we have invested certain individuals and institutions with the authority to watch over the less fortunate—to manage the multitudes of misfortunes, to act as our moral consciences beyond what we, ourselves, might do to ameliorate the situation. In the name of care we have, however, committed a grave sin.

On my way to engaging with street youth for the purposes of collecting data about their experiences before, on, or after the street, I encountered this sin. I didn't know it at first. It hit me all at once. All of a sudden, bits and pieces of stories and reactions, of commitments and comments I had collected over time, spoke to me about the operations operating at levels I had previously not been able to hear—maybe had not wanted to hear. This is the funny thing that happened on the way to my research.

I connected with service providers in my area to apprise them of my research and hoped to develop community partner relationships with some or any of them to facilitate my work. Obviously, I was sure to gain from that connection. I had hoped and believed that the value of my research might be enough of a gain for the agencies to invite me into their domain. I thought that my pursuing a Ph.D. and devoting my energies to understanding youth at risk was the same, or at least philosophically similar, to their commitment to working with and helping kids on the street. I still believe that, or want to, or need to.

My first encounter was with a woman who had worked for many years in a supervisory position in one of the agencies. She had also done research in the area but had recently made a career change. She told me that when she graduated from school, she had decided that she would help ten students as a way of giving back to the process that she had recently been through. I was impressed with the benevolence of the gesture and was relieved to have made it in before her ten-student cut-off. Our conversation was interesting. For the most part she told me about her research and asked little about mine. We met over coffee. One thing she said, however, did strike me. She told me that in order for me to "get" any street kids to talk to me, I had better find a way to give them something in return. She said that "nobody does anything for nothing." I replied politely that I did not want to do that and proceeded to explain why. I stored the comment and remember feeling disappointed that her assumption was that kids don't give freely of themselves. That seemed to be the pervasive belief, tacitly operating but operating nonetheless.

What ideas about benevolence do we have? And what if any effect would these beliefs and assumptions have on the kinds of services we offer to kids? Which philosophical undergirdings drive those services? And are they adequately aligned to honestly cope with the street kids who meet them in the unspoken rules of how one operates in our society?

Sometime later I began to contact agencies to "house" me during my interviewing with street kids. I explained my research goals and assumed that our common desire to help street kids would facilitate the opening of agencies' doors. I called a host of places trying to locate my research and myself, and also to gain an understanding of the city's street topography. I learned that some agencies did not work directly with street kids, and so I moved along in my quest for community partnership. I also discovered that for some agencies, denying me access was due to the overwhelming amount of research already being conducted. Service providers and front-line workers seemed to be distrustful of lofty academic pursuits, and really who could blame them? I conversed about the particular kind of research (i.e., interpretive) that I was committed to, but despite shared values about surveys and the like, some doors were closed and I had to respect that.

From this experience I recognized how academia was negatively located in the consciousness of helping professionals, those working directly with the populations we, academics, seem to want to study. Strange isn't it that we want to examine the lives of individuals as if we are somehow disconnected from the experiences that they are living? I wondered about this and about power relations among professionals. I thought a lot about the act of staking out territories that are claimed and reclaimed by industry and individuals, that are vied for by institutions and agencies, and my expedition into this topography became more complex.

Finally I encountered the agency with which I really wanted to partner. This agency dealt with street kids in a way that would allow me to hang out with the kids and get to know them with the goal of them coming to know me as well. I approached the agency and was immediately met with excitement and enthusiasm by the program director. After a long battle of negotiating academic and ethical clearance for my study, and after an arduous exploration of the various agencies in my city, I felt that my research was about to take off and I would finally get to engage the topic that I had set out to explore. I could hardly contain my excitement.

My first meeting with the agency was thrilling. We talked about street kids and shared ideas about what gaps in service might exist. I explained my research and also my approach in coming to work collaboratively with street kids. I ventured to explain the murky waters of hermeneutic research and described some differences between other kinds of research endeavors and my own. Everything seemed to be clear and on target. I had brought my research proposal for their perusal as well as a shortened and more concise ethics proposal. We were on line. It was explained that the director with whom I met would bring my proposal to a "quality assurance" committee and that if I hadn't heard within a week, I should call to inquire about the project. We shook hands and I left.

The following week I called and was asked to procure the ethics approval form issued by the university. I faxed it. I called again the following week, and again, and again. And then I waited. I was invited to meet with the quality assurance chair and the director of the program to discuss problems with my research proposal. I consented. In the course of this interview, three major issues surfaced: (a) the agency was uncomfortable with the use of pseudonyms as a way of circumventing parental consent regulations even though we all agreed that street kids are situated differently than the norm and therefore require different accommodations; (b) the agency felt that my surname should appear on the covering letter as opposed to only my first name, and in ensuing discussion we agreed that for safety reasons youth workers often do not provide that kind of information, but in my case they were insistent that I be accountable for the research (we also talked about the plethora of phone numbers and contact names required on consent forms as a way of providing assurance that I could be contacted should the need arise); and (c) the agency had agreed that if an adolescent was receiving benefits from the state, their child welfare worker would have to be contacted to give consent to any research participation (this was a requirement of the agency's accreditation). In my work's defense, I explained the legal and ethical positions that the university and I agreed upon. I was asked to provide a copy of the memo written by the university council regarding these matters. I agreed to think about their concerns and get back in touch with them and the following day faxed the memo.

Frantically, I called my supervisory committee to help me negotiate an agreeable solution to this problem. I began to feel more viscerally that the agency did not want me to participate in this kind of research and was making my partnership with them difficult to achieve. One committee member exclaimed that in the interest of my research moving forward that I should accommodate their needs and get on with it.

I thought long and hard about how I could maintain my academic/research integrity and also meet the agency's needs. I was interested in the dance that we had begun and certainly did not understand the multilayeredness of the dance until now.

My next meeting with the agency was scheduled, and I was proud that I had creatively resolved some of the conflicts of which they had made me aware. I proposed that in order to meet their informed consent requirements that we create an additional consent form. In other words, there would be one form to satisfy the university and meet my needs, and another to satisfy their needs. I also suggested that I would contact the social welfare worker to get consent for any kids who shared with me their social welfare status. And here is where the subtext of this experience leaps out in the foreground.

What about research makes it have integrity anyway? What kinds of commitments do we adhere to so that we live out the ethical, philosophical, and practical values imbedded in the approach that we undertake to bring to bear something unique about a phenomenon? Why are we at all interested in the funny thing that happened on the way to this research or any research at all? To my mind, there are multiple texts converging on the terrain that street kids inhabit and they emanate from diverse backgrounds and have divergent intents. Street kids' lives and all the various connections to that phenomenon are so intensely intertwined in the territoriality that street kids stake out for themselves and that which is also modelled for them by the agencies consigned to oversee them. And oversee they do.

My last meeting with this agency shocked me. I recoiled. I felt it. The burden of power and control was immediate, unavoidable, apparent, experienced, tangible. It was the epiphany that opened up a meta-narrative which invests certain characters and imbues certain players with power. It echoes the harsh realities of our modern world and refracts interferences to the status quo. All of a sudden, an additional story emerged about the youth-trade industry and the infrastructure that maintains it.

Technology and the Youth-Trade Industry

If technology is to be understood as "the ensemble of practices by which one uses available resources in order to achieve certain valued ends" (Laswell, cited in Ellul, 1964, 18), and organization itself is technology, then we have created a technologically advanced youth-trade industry, the facets of which are difficult to tease out. I began to wonder how, on the one hand, the job market which is reliant on disenfranchised youth maintains itself, if, on the other hand, the goals of these agencies are to reduce and ultimately to eradicate the number of disenfranchised people. What would this mean in terms of putting themselves out of business? Have the means (technologies) of helping street kids unwittingly become, on occasion, more valued than the end of helping them (T. Pirosok, personal communication, July 2000)? I wondered about how the status quo might get maintained in spite of the good intentions of the workers helping people in need.

> *[Another] aspect of undifferentiated growth, which is inseparable from economic and technological growth is the growth of institutions—from companies and corporations to colleges and universities, churches, cities, governments, and nations. Whatever the original purpose of the institution, its growth beyond a certain size invariably distorts that purpose by making the self-preservation and further expansion of the institution its overriding aim. (Capra, 1982, 220)*

I was afraid that the goal of eradicating poverty, for example, could not really be realized within the framework of the youth trade-industry because if it could, the people who have those jobs would then be ousted. Changing lives seemed to have gotten lost among the other goals, or maybe gained a kind of different goal in the game of dollars and funding.[6]

In my last meeting with the agency I felt the full burden of my research, of my perspective, of myself as an agent in the world, of my commitments, my ethics, and my ideals. Compared to the youth-trade machine, I felt insignificant. The gatekeepers had closed the doors, locking me out. I wondered if there was something else at work that they didn't want me to know. I kept commenting about how it must be for kids trying to disengage from street life through the dense bureaucratic wall that had, as I saw it, been constructed around them. "If it is this hard for me to get in," I asked, "how hard must it be for kids to get out?"

When I returned to the agency, acquiescing to their needs, trying desperately to partner with them, they erected new blockades for me to negotiate. At some point I also realized that the energy in our meetings was hostile, defensive, and uncomfortable. Of course I assumed that it was a personal thing. They didn't like me. They thought I was trouble. Maybe that

---

[6] Even the youth-trade industry has fallen into the market-economy trap, evidenced in a recent publication called "Street Trends: How Today's Alternative Youth Cultures Are Creating Tomorrow's Mainstream Markets" (Lopiano-Misdom & De Luca, 1997). I had to ask if we have no shame or if everything is for sale, including how to market to kids on the street? Is this what we have agreed to? Are these our values?

was true, or maybe they just didn't want me poking around in their business. Whatever the case, I felt unwelcome and uninvited. I assumed the same was true of my research.

I put forward my idea about using multiple consent forms to meet our various needs. They said maybe, but they didn't think it was promising. I agreed that I would pursue informed consent from kids' welfare workers if they made me aware of those relationships. I reassured them that I would be honest and frank with the kids, while pointing out that some kids might not tell me of their welfare status. I suggested that the director and staff of the agency would not necessarily be aware of the kids I was talking with, and so I would need them to trust that I would "follow the rules." Not only did they respond by telling me that I had to ask each kid her or his child welfare situation before any interviewing, they also informed me that, indeed, they would be aware of all my goings and comings since I would be required to provide a list of my participants.

WHAT? Did I hear right? They want me to tell them who I am interviewing? In my surprise I asked, "How about confidentiality?" The response was immediate: "We are the ones who pick up the pieces so we need to know who you're interviewing." I remember talking to them about the need to collaborate in the event that a kid became upset during an interview, about how in such a case involving the staff made perfect sense, and that a part of what I would tell kids about the conditions under which we would talk together included my telling the agency of their involvement should they become upset. I would do all of this to ensure that kids were supported through the process. I agreed to facilitate the connection between participant and staff member to provide any additional support. I also stated that I would be able to debrief stuff with the kids, at least to some degree, and that I thought in the course of the interviews some of that might happen anyway. They asked me to role play what I would say to kids about my role as a researcher. I was on trial. It was a performance. I was confused by their wanting me to separate my therapist self from my researcher self, from any of the other selves that inhabit me. I thought that to be strange. I did my best to advocate for the kids, for their voices, for myself, and for my research. But the answer was still no. A resounding "we are in control and have to know who you are interviewing" was the bottom line. I decided to move on, to explore the other issues with this agency, and to put what I had just heard aside until I had more time to think.

I felt sad, disappointed, disillusioned. I felt defeated in what I perceived to be the economy of the street. I felt controlled and marginalized, disempowered and angry. Ideals erupted before me that I had not anticipated. I had met another test of integrity. I hoped for strength in my convictions.

The conversation continued. I began to understand that I was not going to be able to partner with this agency, that the fit was not what I had hoped. Still, I maintained a brave face (though I wanted to cry) and made sure I was hearing what they were saying. "So let me understand the landscape here," I said. "Hypothetically, let's say I meet a kid here, I tell them, in the course of explaining my research to them, that I will contact their child welfare worker to get informed consent and that the agency will be aware of their participation in the study. Say a kid declines my offer, doesn't want to participate. Let's imagine that six months later I meet the same kid at a coffee shop downtown, and the kid says that she/he is ready to talk. "What..." As I recall, I didn't need to finish the hypothetical scenario because it was made abundantly clear that if a kid declines to interview under the rules of this particular agency, then they are "disqualified" from my study for life.

WHAT? That was certainly not the answer I expected, but I guess I was not terribly surprised. "Who are you," I thought, and "whose interests are you protecting? Who gave you this kind of control?" "Who says," as one of my supervisors suggested, "that kids cannot change their minds?" What is this about? Why such tight constraints? Who's afraid of what? What is there to uncover? Why did these doors close on me? How would these rules of conduct be perceived by kids and how might they undermine the spaces for voice that I am trying to create for street kids' narratives? What is operating tacitly behind what we are seeing?

I met with my committee, informed them of the agency's conditions, and wrote a "thank you but no thank you" letter explaining the conflict of interest apparent in our two approaches. I was careful to be respectful and appreciative. I did not feel that way at all, and I think they were just as happy not to engage with me.

Getting to the Street

The process of gaining access to street kids by myself was intimidating. I am an outsider after all. I cannot pretend to be otherwise. As a consequence of my dealings with the agency, I found myself in the middle of winter, trying to establish myself on the street. At the beginning, there was trauma. I had lived through a battle at the university about informed consent; I had been disappointed by the agency during the previous four months or so, and I was weary before getting my feet on the ground of my research.

How do these experiences speak about, echo, or resemble the phenomenon that I wanted to understand? I was swimming in a sea of resistance; I was caught in webs I hadn't foreseen. Upon reflection, I wonder to what extent my swirling was/is an aspect of the topic itself? (D. Jardine, personal communication, May 1998)

I continued visiting the street (meaning downtown) over the next few months, making a few contacts but not really being able to connect with kids. I visited another agency that was willing to help, but the population they were serving was inappropriate for my study. I floated around, feeling frustrated and lonely, tired and defeated. The timing was off. Mid-winter is not the time to find and connect with street kids. The weather is a significant determinant of how much action there is on the street. My efforts during these months were futile. I was out of the loop.

Getting acquainted with the street scene for kids started to happen the following summer. I would hang around downtown, still intimidated and shy about approaching kids. It was hard getting connected to street kids; it was foreign, and strange, and uncomfortable. I was connecting with a few kids, but I was not becoming entrenched or known on the street in the way that I needed to. Late in July, after weeks of walking the downtown core, it was suggested to me that I paint a T-shirt advertising my research study as a way to break the ice (T. Pirosok, personal communication, July 1998). I did. My T-shirt read: Street kids speak—to tell your story talk to me.[7] On August 14th, I had my first conversation with a bunch of kids who had noticed my T-shirt and initiated a conversation with me. I was finally there.

---

[7] See Appendix II.

Chapter Three

Panhandling in Place

In the previous chapter I described how I came to the topic and went to the street. I told the tales of preparing for my research and the trials of gaining access to kids on the street. In the following chapters, I will attempt to show you what I learned about life on the street for kids and, more, what I learned about resilience and youth, about marginalization and society, about voice, about power, and about possibilities. This terrain is complex and replete with nuances that continue to emerge. It reflects back on itself in a million ways. Its paths are bountiful—some lead us deep into the experiences of kids on the street, some lead into the core of ourselves, but mostly we are led into the tensions that live in between. All at the same time, this book is about the kids on the street, about the values we live by, about doing research, and about the web of interrelated issues and institutions mingling in the confluence of the narratives of kids living on the street.

Dancing with the Data

Before I begin to tell you the stories of the street, I must first tell you a little bit about how the following two chapters came into being. Although I continually comment on my own learning and questioning of the data throughout these chapters (as hermeneutic inquiry suggests), I think it is useful to lay out here the process that brought me to understand something new about the experiences of life on the street for kids. As you will see, homeless kids had a lot to say about their experiences on the street. I was amazed at some of the topics that we talked about and was taken aback by some of the connections they made about the circumstances of their lives. I was confronted with the enormity of what the kids had said about their lives on the street. During my time on the street, I kept notes, listened attentively to what I was being told, and reflected on the multiple levels of experience the kids were sharing with me about their lives on the street. As will become apparent, kids spoke with me both about the specific aspects of their street experiences, as well as about how those specific experiences connected to, or were a part of, the larger systems with which they intersected. Thus, for example, the rules of panhandling are explored in this chapter, whereas in the next chapter, panhandling is situated within a greater sociopolitical context. In other words, I begin in the particularities of what the kids told me about their experiences on the street, and from there I spiral out, interpreting, connecting, and incorporating the larger systems to which the kids also spoke. Right from the outset, my conversations with kids on the street were simultaneously about the specific and about the general, about the personal and about the political. In these next chapters I attempt to show an ever-expanding domain of understanding which continually explicates more and more about kids and their lives on the street. Gallagher (1992) comments that "[t]he more movement in the circle, the larger the circle grows, embracing and expanding the contexts that throw more light upon the parts" (59), the better the interpretation will be for showing the whole.

In order to propel my understanding of street kids' lives through the expanding nature of hermeneutic inquiry, I have tried to engage the hermeneutic circle to renovate whatever I can bring to bear on the topic. I have heard, listened to, and questioned kids' accounts of street life in the spirit of "good will." Gadamer's conception of "good will" suggests that

> one does not go about identifying the weakness of what another person says in order to prove that one is always right, but one seeks instead as far as possible to strengthen the other's viewpoint so that what the other person has to say becomes illuminating. (Gadamer, 1989 cited in Risser, 1997, 167)

Since my understanding of the "street kid world" evolves through concentric levels of ever-expanding interpretations, Chapters Three and Four should be read as incomplete parts of a greater whole. Chapter Three focuses on panhandling as one of the central experiences of life on the street for kids, weaving its way from the rules of panhandling to street life as a site for contested identities. In Chapter Four, panhandling is considered in terms of its positioning on the street and its political and economic meanings within the broader culture. Both chapters speak to the experiences of street kids, and both chapters are components of the greater texture of what I learned about life on the street for kids. I tried to honor my commitment to move between the parts and the whole in building the interpretation that you will now read and hope that what is unfamiliar will emerge as illuminated and illuminating.

The Set-Up

On my first trip back to the street, in the month of July, I chose to park my car at a nearby public transit station and ride the train into the downtown. I was feeling intimidated, unsure, and unsteady about the process on which I was embarking. I wasn't sure how I was going to meet kids by myself; I wasn't sure about how I would fit into their geography, their landscape, their space. I wasn't sure about much and I understood that experience to be part of the "emergent design" nature of this research. A friend agreed to accompany me so that I could become familiar with the street scene with a bit of reinforcement. We arrived at the station, bought our fares, and boarded the first train downtown. Our plan was to walk around and get a sense of the space that kids inhabit in the downtown core.

The first thing I noticed when I got into the train car was a placard that read "Make real change with your spare change...Giving to panhandlers doesn't solve a thing."[8] I wondered what that was about, questioning whose interests were being served by that sign and what the intention of it was. Revisited by familiar feelings of disappointment in what I perceived to be the "establishment's" attempt to erase homelessness from the city landscape, I recalled my work with kids on the street in another major city and recalled my frustration with what I thought was a predominantly narrow view of how kids come to be on the street in the first

---

[8] See Appendix III.

place. I read that sign as a cultural artifact that asked me to believe that my only civic responsibility was to support the institutions that have been charged with looking after the needy, the homeless, the poor. It was testimony, I thought, to the growing need to eliminate any negative or uncomfortable experiences for people making their way downtown to shop, or eat, or work.

The transit car I rode was both the literal and metaphoric vehicle that took me to the street, that set a certain aspect of this inquiry in motion, that delivered me to the site where street kids live. I wondered how many other interpretations there could be about the subtext of that sign and how that poster served to set us up to interact with the reality of homelessness in particular ways. Perhaps signs like that give us permission to ignore what happens around us in the inner city. Perhaps signs like that assuage our feelings of guilt about poverty, assuring us that there are agencies out there to help. Who had paid for these signs? Over time, I noted that these signs were in every car on the train; they were also in every downtown parking lot, prominently displayed near elevators, and stairs, and entrances. What authority was instructing us and for what purpose? I made a mental note.

Some six weeks after that first train ride downtown, I had my first "formal" conversation with a group of street kids. I was sitting outside at the McDonald's on the pedestrian mall which functioned as the gathering and connecting site for street kids. It was a warm, late afternoon in August. A group of four street kids invited me to sit with them after remarking on my T-shirt. They said that they had noticed me a few days earlier and that they were going to be sitting there for awhile "panning." I explained what I was doing and what my research was all about, and they appeared excited about having an opportunity to tell their stories. I told them that I hoped to write a book one day to help get their words out to a wider audience. I told them I wanted to be a conduit and that I wanted to hear about how they make meaning from their experiences as street kids. I felt like there was an immediate sense of mutuality between us. I approached them as valued commentators on their street experiences, and I believe they sensed my authentic respect for whatever they were going to say about their lives. I didn't offer them anything monetary. There was no promise of material reward—they didn't even ask! As it turned out, this conversation proved to be monumental in my understanding of street kids and their experiences on the street. It introduced me to the harshness of sitting on the ground and asking people for money. Whatever I had thought about street life before changed in an instant.

Rhythms of the Street

There is a clicking. A rhythmic, healthy, unthwarted sound of expensive shoes
    that echo click, click, clicking down the mall.
Reverberating rhythms of shoes, and the feet who fill them, attached to bodies
    —well-appointed, mid-50ish wo[men] in suits, busily clicking by.

Down on the ground, sitting on the street,
        the sound of those shoes is especially loud.

Deafening...
    Different from the slow, broken, sloughing sounds
    singing from the tired feet of the homeless.
Aimless rhythms—rhythms of contrast, rhythms of the street

Identity Identified

An important interjection. Before I continue turning in the hermeneutic cycles and circles of understanding, casting nets into how street life is interpreted by kids, by me, and in the literature, I would like to offer a map or guideline to aid in our journeying through this topic together. In inquiring about the lives and experience of street kids, I imagined that I was going to hear about the things that constitute their existences on the street and the meanings they ascribe to their lives. In asking them to tell me their stories, I was positioned to hear assertions about selves and identities since at least part of what they were going to be telling me was about themselves and their lives. As I conversed with the kids, and also with the data in the renovating cycles of the hermeneutic endeavor, I understood more and more about how street kids' identities were being forged through what they said about themselves, others, and society, as well as how they were physically positioned in the site of the street. There are, I'm certain, hundreds of visions of what the self might be, and those diverging vantage points differentially affect the way in which we take up an issue, the way we interpret a scene, the way we might read into or onto the subjectivities that we encounter, even though these entities are permanently in motion. So, before you read about the evolving identities of street kids, I offer my evolving conception of what the self is, hoping that it may aid both in your understanding of me, and in my explication of street kids and street life.

The self to which I refer throughout this text is multiply constituted. That means that there are a plethora of facets to the self that I understand to be imbedded in the organic fabric of life and living. I understand the self as embodied, in relation, as agent, in practice, as reflexive, as negotiated, as seen, and as enslaved. It is to these aspects of self I will briefly speak. I'm sure that I haven't covered all the parts of what the self is, how the self comes to be, how the self comes to act or gets acted upon in the world, but these perspectives of self will nevertheless illuminate how I conceive of the many mingling aspects that make up the self and ultimately the selves that are on the street.

To frame the discussion of the diverse facets of the self, let me first lay down a continuum on which my understanding of the self lies. On one end of the continuum is the self who has total agency. This self is not affected by other, by society, by power, and is only self-referential. On the other end of the continuum is the self who is passive, agency-less, at the mercy of the structure which programs and influences the self's existence. This self has no choice, has no inner reflexive capability, is only a docile vesicle. It is not at either of these two extremes that I envision the constituted self, but rather in the tensions and strains that exist between them. My understanding of self and identity is that they are both products and producers of agency and docility, that they arise in the negotiated spaces and power configurations that both impinge and afford their development, and that the dialectical flow between the poles temporarily locate them somewhere on the continuum of agency and docility.

As embodied.

[W]e use our bodies for grounding personal identity in ourselves and in recognizing it in others. We use other bodies as points of reference in relating to other material things. We use our bodies for the assignment of all sorts of roles, tasks, duties, and strategies. We use our bodies for practical action. We use our bodies for the expression of moral judgements...We use

human bodies for the management of the people so embodied. We use our own bodies and those of others to command the cosmos. We use our bodies as message boards, and their parts as succinct codes.(Harré, 1991 cited in Pile & Thrift, 1995, 6)

I offer the embodied self as the self of the corporeal. Above are some of the ways that our bodies both cast us into certain spaces and also let us break free of others. What we understand about ourselves and the world is mediated in part through our embodied experiences. There is no chance for the self to be configured in the head, separated and severed from the body. The embodied self is partly a body that is "a site of cultural consumption, a surface to be written on" (Pile & Thrift, 1995, 7), but it is also a site for power and action. The embodied self struggles in between the extremes of agency and docility and "provides us with a way of access to the world..." (Merleau-Ponty, 1962, cited in Pile & Thrift, 1995, 6). The embodied self is the holistic self and is a facet of the self that both inscribes and is inscribed into the complexes of identity.

   In relation, negotiation, and reflection. *The self understood as a being-in-relation refers to the dialectical relationships that are forged between the self and itself, the self and other, and the self in the world, including whatever combinations and permutations are found in the arrangements within and between those islands of contact. In the context of the continuum between agency and docility, the self negotiates space in the diversity of coordinates found in the in-betweens of the binary opposites of total freedom and total oppression. Layers of complexity are further compounded when the relational and negotiated self also intersects with the manifold complications and power relations imbedded in aspects of class, race, gender, privilege, power, and so on. Relations and negotiations constitute location, meaning, and power for the embodied self which is constantly calibrating how, where, and in what manner identity can come to be.*

   As agent, in practice, as enslaved. *The embodied self is an agent. But agency is not free from the regimes of power, privilege, and circumstance that mitigate our experiences in this life. That means that identity comes from agents choosing to act as well as from agents being acted upon. The* *relative freedom or constraint afforded to the subject is determined both by the limits and boundaries in which the self can operate and by understanding if and how hidden agendas and silent subjugations operate in context. "Agency, if it is anything, is a precarious achievement" (Law, 1994, cited in Pile & Thrift, 1995, 35), because agency is always being restricted by the arrangements and interactions between the self and the world. The tentativeness of agency is part and parcel of the appreciation that the self/identity is an evolving, dynamic, and dialectical constellation that can only be temporarily mapped based on the meanings and power relations that are operating at any given time.*

"[T]he subject's understanding comes from the ceaseless flow of conduct, conduct which is future oriented" (Pile & Thrift, 1995, 27). The active self has "a generative, creative capacity to understand" (Pile & Thrift, 1995, 28). This understanding is manifest in the dialectic of the self in practice, in action, as agent. But depending upon impediments which may hamper the continual flow of action of the self, the self is always at risk for becoming enslaved, captured, arrested, overcome, or overpowered.

As seen in scene. *This aspect of the self is related to how we come to know ourselves by visual cues and clues, in places and spaces. This is the part of the self that is gazed upon and is also the self who is the gazer. Situated, constituted, negotiated, and embodied, the self is an agent of seeing and being seen in scene.*

> *Each dimension of seeing invokes differently a different kind of space between the person who looks and the object that looks back: there is a position, distance, and an orientation to the look, which specifies a particular space of meaning and power: this space is neither isolated nor abstract; this space both contains and refuses an infinite number of invocations of meaning and power; this space is constitutive of the visual practice, it is staging and integrating the lines of power and meaning between the look and the look-back. (Pile & Thrift, 1995, 46)*

In these gazes there is no neutral stare; similarly, there is no neutral space in which the stare comes. These visual understandings are connected to everything that the self learns and teaches. Sight is negotiated as a site for contestation.

In all these ways the identity is contested and remade; selves are emerging, changing, and evolving. People resist and receive; they offer and counter; they shift and change in the web of intersections that make up the complexities of their lives as humans living together on this planet. My understanding of self is that it is generative, constituted, temporal, dialectic, seen, embodied, locatable but also somewhat ethereal, meaning-making, complex, and contested. As is evidenced above, there are a number of ways to understand how people come to be, how they come to know themselves and others, how they are situated and situate themselves in places and spaces and relationships. People's identities, therefore, evolve through their relationships to themselves, in their contact with others, and in the ways in which they are positioned or position themselves within the greater social fabric. Understanding self and identity in terms of the continuum of agency and docility affords a complex and rich perspective through which the facets of self can be understood. Each aspect of ourselves can be active but activity is also determined by power relations, privilege, and other hindrances that we may not even be able to name.

> *Encounters, then, appear to offer a tangled web of interaction between people, as they are mapped into power-ridden discursively-constituted identities, where such interactions place individuals in complex positions in relation to power and meaning, where power and meaning are policed through bi-polar opposites, but where power and meaning cannot be contained by the violence of bisection. (Pile & Thrift, 1995, 44)*

This explication of what I understand the self to be is offered so that throughout the following chapters street kids and their lives will be able to be appreciated in a myriad of ways. It is not offered as a theoretical measure on which to judge street kids but rather as a tool in understanding their experiences in a multifaceted way. Pile and Thrift (1995), the source for much of my understanding of this open, dialectical perspective of self, comment that the literature on self, identity, and subjectivity is "too academic, in that it reads the writings of intellectuals on body, self, person, identity, and subject..." (371). They suggest that there is "still a gulf between theory and much of the work on everyday usages of body, self, person, identity, and subject..." (Pile & Thrift, 1995, 371). And so, in our wayfinding through the complexities that face kids on the street and the interpretations that we both offer (i.e., the kids and I), these facets of a generative and discursively constituted self will hopefully enable us to encounter what they said about their lives and the conditions of the street in an illuminated way.

Panhandling as the Embodiment of Street Life for Kids

That first interview touched upon panhandling and many of its corollary interpretations and meanings. In fact, most of the subsequent conversations I had with street kids broached that subject to some degree or another. To my amazement, much of what street kids spoke about was reflected in how they understood themselves, others, and society through their daily toil, their vocation, their work, that is, the embodied task of asking passersby for change. They were thoughtful and contemplative about what this experience meant for them and how it shaped and determined how they understood the world around them. During this particular conversation there was a constant starting and stopping of discussion. In conversations dotted with a continual "Spare any change, sir, so I can get home?" these kids spoke to me about what it means to panhandle. "Why don't you give *me* some?" a passerby snippily jibes when asked for change. "I would if I could but I can't. That's why I'm asking you," Jar boldly responds. I ask them, "So do you think that lots of people, like a guy like that for example, does he understand your predicament or is he…" and the chorus of voices races to fill in the gaps of my understanding. "The guy that just walked by (pointing to a nicely dressed businessman)…Some people understand, some people don't. That guy, I doubt if he does," Bobby says. Neil muses, "He might have a little idea of what it's about," and again Bobby answers "He might even know but he doesn't care." A fourth voice enters the fray. Jem says:

> Like I would like to take some of the people who have golden spoons in their mouth, all the time, their entire life, and make them go absolutely bankrupt, have their family disown them, or kick them out and say, "You know what? I don't like you, I hate you, I wish I never had you." Have your friends who you were so high class and now you're down below, they all turn on you too. I want to put them on the streets for a night or two and see how they like it. Because you know I've got girls, some girls they walk past me and they've got their nose up in the air, and they're like, "No, I don't want to spare any

change for you, you're lower than I am," right. And it's just like, go along the street... (Jem, 08/14/98)

"We're all humans, we all have feelings," exclaims Neil. "Exactly. I'm just as equal as you. You may have more money than me but I've got more respect and more friends than you do" (Jem, 08/14/98).

A while later, I was sitting in the same location amidst a flurry of street kid action, interviewing a fifth kid who had come to join his buddies. A woman walked by and mumbled something barely intelligible: "...no, you're not my kids, I have two," she angrily and venomously muttered between clenched teeth, almost—but not so convincingly—under her breath. What was that woman trying to convey? What need was she meeting by jeering at the kids? I felt stunned and in an odd way personally affronted. I asked the group what they thought that was about? "I don't know why she said that. All I said was have a nice day," Bobby said raising his hands, palms open to the sky, shrugging his shoulders as if to question her behavior as well. There seemed to be a hint of embarrassment among the kids about being the recipients of this unsolicited verbal assault. But embarrassment doesn't describe it fully. Maybe shame might be more accurate, yes, shame mixed with helplessness, complicated by a dose of indignation for what they habitually live on the street. An introductory proof of the conditions of street life for kids, this was like a public confession of their circumstance, as if to say, "See what I mean? This is what we put up with." "What do you think she meant?" I asked again. "It means that she's a fucking bitch" (Bohdi, 08/14/98).

From that moment onward something changed in my understanding of kids' experiences on the street. From that moment onward I was attuned to the tensions that inhabit the spaces in between people and especially in between these people. The space that I had encountered, that the kids named, that felt heavy in the balance of where street kids and mainstream societies meet, began to tell me a story of opposites, of universes miles away from each other, of conflicted and confused battlefields where selves and souls struggle to survive. It was in this tension that the kids' conversations lived, in the strains and pulls of contradictory worlds, in the embodied discomfort of the street clashing constantly with the regular rhythms of mainstream life that I found myself with them—uncomfortable and confused—with them and their experiences.

And so, life on the street for kids centered literally and figuratively in the geography of the street. Music and noise, the hustle of the city, and the din of constant chatter, interruptions, sensory traffic, and regular interchanges among friends, acquaintances, and strangers created a congested space alive with its own sense of order and its own sense of time. This is where we met and spoke about street life. This is where they invited me to be with them. This is where they taught me.

When I began writing about this experience, I quickly learned about the difficulties in setting experiences into expression. How could I ever transcend the constraints of temporality, the boundaries of time, space, and lived experience? I wanted to cogently construct a narrative from the profundity of what the kids shared with me, and offer the story as I needed to tell it, as the kids hoped I would, as it itself, with all its possibilities, needed to emerge from the endless pages of transcriptions, as it echoed inside of me from memories etched in permanent and powerful ways, but the complexity of doing it was and is so terribly complicated. In writing about what the kids told me, in attempting a million sentences and starting over countless times, I realized I would be confronting a central and perennial problem. There is no way. There is no defined and linear path to follow. The vastness and complexity of people's lives lie in the very meandering gullies and paths that confound life's choices and ideas, that amble around in life's thoughts and beliefs. I knew that my task was to do it, to show you, to take you along the journey, and engage you transformatively as I progressed. But was I going to deliver it all in a way that made sense? Gadamer (1995) says that "writing is a kind of alienated speech, and its signs need to be transformed back into speech and meaning. Because the meaning has undergone a kind of self-alienation through being written down, this transformation back is the real hermeneutical task" (393). Lee (1998) says "[t]he impasse of writing that is problematic to itself is transcended only when the impasse becomes its own subject, when writing accepts and enters and names its own conditions as it names the world" (21). This is the problematic I was feeling and facing. The convergence of ideas and hopes and ideals was deafening, paralyzing me, scaring me. This was an awesome task to engage, not only because of what lay in the balance for me, but rather because there were kids counting on me out there. Their hope and their scorn rested uncomfortably on my shoulders, looking over me, after me, through me. It is ultimately for them that their words must surface, but for you and me, it's simply our only hope.

And so, in the following pages you will read what I have come up with, settled on, resigned to. "[E]verything depends on the art of writing," Gadamer says (1995, 393), and so in spite of the difficulties of wanting to say everything all at once—to show every tension, to connect all the tendrils—I decided to begin with the simple and concrete, and move through to the complex and abstract (as if there is anything simple or concrete about the story of someone's life). I borrowed from my heritage, heeding the ancient wisdom of Torah interpretation that acknowledges the multifarious voices that reverberate simultaneously in utterances, levels all at once leading us here and there in our understandings. I hoped that I could be sufficiently open to allow the complicated polyphony of voices to emerge such that the intricate dance of a topic's own cadence could be heard (Lee, 1998).

Rules of Panhandling

One of the ways street kids connected with me in talking about their lives was to describe the rules of the game to me. Like the initiation of a new club member, Neil, Bobby, Jem, Jar, and Bohdi oriented me to the centrality of panning and the intricacies therein. These regulations served as a way to explain to me how the street works.

> That's why I sit here and even if someone gets rude with me and says, "Oh why don't you get a fucking job?" "Oh, excuse me sir, do you have one that you can spare then?" And even if someone doesn't say anything, I say, "Thanks, have a nice day." You know, I'm polite about it. (Neil, 08/14/98)

Bobby reflects on how that kind of politesse is manifest in their treatment of the physical space of the street they inhabit. "You know what—when we sit here and we panhandle, we have pop and stuff like that, you notice when we leave there's no garbage sitting…" Neil jumps in again, "Yeah, we usually clean our spot very well." "We clean our stuff up all of the time.

And then I see people walk out of McDonald's, rich guys, you know they're rich, they're wearing a Rolex and a thousand-dollar suit…and they just throw their stuff on the ground," Jar concurs. "I watched one guy yesterday; he was right beside the garbage can and threw it on the ground. People don't care," Bobby concludes. "We have respect. We have respect for the people" (Jem, 08/14/98). *I noticed the remark about status and wondered how the Rolex watch was connected to being careless about garbage and how status was connected to respect?* The kids continue.

> Yeah, and people don't realize that, people always think because there are those nasty dickheads [referring to other street kids] that look at you when you say no, and they go, "Fine, fuck you then." I hate those guys. They give us a bad name and make it hard for us to get out of the city, very hard [i.e., to make sufficient cash to move on]. We're never like that. We're always polite, always nice. And most of us are, most of us are *really* nice. (Bobby)

There seemed to be something more to what I was being told about kids' cleanliness and respect for the physicality of the street. I wondered whether it was only about picking up one's garbage before vacating an area, or if something else was being asserted by telling me about how clean and polite they are? Were they telling me something about who they are? About their values?

The rules of engagement seemed complex, and I knew that there was more to uncover. I was new to the scene and was learning about the circumstances of the street as a neophyte. *Why is politesse so important to name I wonder? Is it because being polite proves that you are human? Normal? Nice? More like the rest of us? Does it get you further in your job as a panhandler? Breitbart (1998) contends that street kids are "using public space to contest preconceptions about themselves, and their lives, goals and aspirations" (308). She suggests that kids' use of public space through street art, design, and performance is often about "reclaiming a space for themselves in urban life" (Breitbart, 1998, 308). Perhaps the same is true in the enactment of panhandling? Echoed in what the kids were telling me, I noted that there was more to think about in terms of public space and kids' locality in/on it.* Meanwhile the kids were asserting that they are not disrespectful, that they are considerate, and that people have them all wrong. Recapitulating again and again the in-betweenness of their experiences on the street, kids testify about their identities and ideals, about selves and experiences that are incongruent with the mythology of who and what street kids are.[9] I was attuned to listen for more.

> But here [referring to the street], I mean yeah, it's a completely different set of rules like, and they're all rules that people obey just because they know that it makes sense. Like panhandlers, I mean, almost everybody that I panhandle with, they don't ask people with children. They don't ask people with children for spare change even if they can afford to give it away, because a lot of them have come from really poor families, where their parents are really poor, and having kids, you know, it takes a lot of money. And it's just like I don't ask homeless people, well, of course, I don't ask homeless people, I don't ask disabled people or really elderly people because I know they need their money, like a lot, and they don't have any to spare. But you know, it's just rules like that or you know like, in a place where you sleep you don't break glass all over it, and like the places where you hang out, you know, you don't take a dump on it and stuff like that. It's just like common rules that people know and that people will just abide by because, I don't know... (Mike, 10/05/98)

Because this is how kids adjust to living on the street and living with each other. You learn the rules because the rules make sense. They're practical; they help you survive. Mike articulates how diverse populations need and use money differentially, and expresses a moral ethic in his panhandling practice by naming those from whom panhandlers see fit to ask for money. But I imagine that there is more infused in street governance than simply knowing who to ask for money and who not to, but I'm not sure what it is

---

[9] The literature on street kids is remarkably silent on issues of kids' ethical, moral, or value systems. The rules governing street conduct in terms of street kids' social living arrangements or connections to the mainstream are almost completely absent from the current body of scholarly literature (for exceptions see, for example, Carlen [1996], Plympton [1997], or Hagan & McCarthy [1997] for a discussion of street families and life on the street respectively). This lacuna might be the case because positively oriented presentations of the lives of homeless youth, including the way they conceive of their world with regard to ethical, moral, political, and social codes, have not been undertaken. It may also be due to the traditional research focus on concrete aspects of street life, or might be a result of a predominant, preconceived mainstream belief (i.e., by researchers, adults, etc.) that street life and street kids are essentially maladaptive (Lundy, 1995). In other words, street life and street youth have been immutably conceived of as "a complex and persistent social problem" (Bradley, 1997, 3) and have been studied within that framework by social scientists who have been trained to pathologize (Carlen, 1996).

yet.

Beyond the rules that define the parameters of panning, I wondered how these guidelines represented codes of behavior or ethics of the street. I understood that these were the simple details to which they could speak that, in turn, could help teach me. These rules seemed to be reflective of how kids live together on the street and how they make their living panhandling, but these rules also led me to believe that life on the street is more complicated than just having rules.

Right from the outset, my conversations with kids on the street exposed me to what I perceived to be the cruel and thoughtless behavior of adults toward panhandling kids. I was astounded by people's reactions to kids on the street that very first day and began to search for more comprehensive answers to piece this puzzle together. Why do street kids engender such vehemence? What makes the existence of street kids and people's interactions with them so complicated? Is the status quo somehow being perpetuated, and if so, by whom, and why? Why aren't things different for street kids? How are kids being marginalized and further oppressed by their daily experiences on the street? What long-term effects to self and soul are permanently imprinted on these kids from the endless abuses assailing them while they live on the street? Questions were coming to me in an endless flow, spurred on by the relentless confessions of kids about their circumstances on the street and my experience of being on the street with them. They were talking about positioning and social class issues; they were telling me about politics and being hated, about lack of resources and isolation. Everything began to connect in a web of interrelated concepts and ideas. I was completely overwhelmed. I was able to begin to answer some of my questions while others had to wait in abeyance for me to figure my way through what the kids were sharing with me. I had to be patient and know that I couldn't develop an understanding in one fell swoop.

Two young women related to me some of the things shouted to them as they occupied the public spaces of the street. Sarah (08/17/98) described her experience of panning this way. She said, "[I]t's hard. Like people say, like, when we panhandle, they say like 'Fucking get a job' or 'You're street rats and you're just shit'" (08/14/98). Just shit? What does that mean? Zena (08/24/98) offered her account of panhandling by revealing to me the degrading assaults of men passing by.

> [T]hey're worthless [speaking about what mainstream folk think of street kids]. And people tell you to get a job all the time, and people throw money at you. I've had a guy, like no offense to the tape recorder or anything, but two times I've had two corporate assholes, I asked one, "Spare some change for a bite to eat today sir," and he said, "I have something you can bite on" [as she motions to her genitalia]. And I had another guy, I said, "Excuse me sir, could you possibly be able to spare some change for a bite to eat today," and he said, "Show me your pussy first."

I was arrested in my tracks, amazed by what I'd heard, what she had found important to tell me about, what was memorable about her experiences on the street. Piety and pity—"For sale only little girl." "Change only when you've been undone, when I've reduced you, disrobed your dignity, peeled you for my pleasure. Change is a commodity little girl and so are you." She excuses the vulgarities of the street as if to shelter me from the brutality of what she's lived, to save me from what has toughened her, and slapped her, and made her real.

Again I picked up on the reference to socioeconomic class, and I began to wonder about the divisions that separate street kids from others. Heavily aligned in the very economic fabric of our society "corporate assholes" (Zena, 08/24/98) stood out for me, jumped away from Zena's description of her life as a street kid because her characterization seemed to be made pointedly, with purpose. I wondered if, in addition to being marginalized and subjected to adults' poor opinions of and contemptuous treatment of street kids, the experiences of the street were also somehow tied up in larger issues of money, power, and privilege. Zena's comments seemed to cast "corporate assholes" into a particular camp, a camp that both set her apart from them, and also set me apart from her.

That realization changed everything for me. I had lost the person that I was before. My status as an outsider became, in that very instant, my sullied identity. Money, privilege, and position were all mine, and they bumped and chaffed me at every turn; they gnawed and burned in me as I crept silently away from the street into my car, into my home, into my fridge, into my wallet, into my books, and my musings, and my judgments. Bourgeois, liberal crap I concluded. What was this research about anyway? Who was I helping and in what way? How could this research be different? I was mining the kids' resources for my own gain, wasn't I? I was adamant about not commodifying my relationship with the kids by paying them or providing coupons for them as other researchers had done, my small proof that I believe in these kids and in their benevolence. But how was I going to be different? How could I prove to myself, and to them, that I was with them even though my life was separated from theirs? Was that a possibility, or are the lines of caste and class sufficiently sharp to sever any mingling of the species? I felt like the lines were indeed sharp, and I was saddened about how separated I felt from them. My answers were not clear and my discomfort visceral. That same day I wrote this in my journal.

> *Upon leaving the street I walked into the Bay [a department store]. My senses were confronted and affronted by the grotesque differences separating the two worlds of downtown, differences separated only by transparent glass doors enclosing the Bay. I was dizzy.*
>
> *Every fiber of my body experienced the contrast. My eyes awakened to bright, carefully placed and designed lighting, my body relaxed as I entered into the establishment—literally and figuratively. I was surrounded by the familiar and it felt safe, and clean, and antiseptic.*
>
> *My nose breathed deeply, breathed odors that anoint and delight the senses of the wealthy, or the cared-for, or both.*
>
> *All I could think of was abundance. Greed. Extravagance. Excess. Decadence. Luck. But alas, this is the world we live in. Riches to taunt and tempt. Only separated by transparent glass doors. (Me, 08/24/98)*

From the rules of panhandling to an ever-widening understanding of what was going on for kids on the street, I wanted to understand more about the experiences of kids in their lives on the street. I had some clues now about rules, positioning, and economics, and I was ready for more.

The Good, The Bad, The Ugly, and The Twinkies in Between

As I came to understand, through our conversations, the polarities of street life for kids are represented in the multiple interpretations of their panhandling experiences. For some kids panning is an opportunity to live out the romantic view of the free, boundless bohemian; for others, the experience is degrading and debilitating, and calls into question the way that they view themselves as street dwellers.

Manifest in this daily toil, being a street kid can represent a kind of hippie identity that in itself speaks to a greater political consciousness. Neil says:

> [P]anhandling really took another swing. Panhandlers started coming out of the woodwork in the early nineties. And before it was the sixties. And what it is, is a cultural thing. It rotates. It happens over again…Panhandling is back in. Hacky-sack is back in. Pot smoking is bigger than ever now. It's the sixties all over again. (Neil, 08/14/98)

And in that, Neil tries to open a space for his own coming to terms with his life and vocation. Making sense of his life, Neil tries to clear a small space for the experiences of street life to be read as positive. He referentially conjures up images of an historical period that celebrated peace and freedom, love, hope, and community—images of a time that set youth against establishment, that named oppression and magnified desires for liberation. The sixties, equally a time of turmoil, derision, war, and chaos, is nostalgically and romantically invoked as the cultural referent for the peace and love movement and the signifier of his perspective of the street. I didn't ask Neil to elaborate on how his experience of the street was like the sixties, or if it was, but love and community, peace and freedom were concepts that surfaced over and over and over. Bohdi told me that "traveling has changed [his] life." He said, "I've learned shit that I can't learn in any city anywhere. I've learned to talk to people without being afraid of them. [B]eing on the streets is hard sometimes, man, but it's worth it. We're doing what real teenagers do; we don't have a place to call home." Bohdi suggested that being on the street is about "connection. It's an emotional and spiritual bond, it's a thing of respect" (08/14/98).

I was hearing positive reflections about what the street experience could mean. In addition to how those explanations could come from a position of rationalizing away a set of bad circumstances and experiences, I wondered if perhaps understanding street kids' moves away from normative mainstream pathways might be broadened to include reconceptualizations of youth as traveler, freedom-seeker, or resilient, conscientious objector (see, for example, Carlen, 1996; Lundy, 1995; Mayers & Olafson, 1997; Ruddick, 1998). Given what I'd heard, I took up the possibility that there might be something beautiful happening on the street for youth despite the turmoil and pain that comes with it as Neil and Bohdi suggested. I wondered about how personal strength might develop through the experience of being a street kid. Maybe there is more to being a street kid than being a bum. Can we allow ourselves to imagine that the pedagogy of the street may also be fertile, valuable, and full of possibility?

At the very least, from the accounts of the kids that I'd heard from, the experience of being a street kid presented as being complicated and confounded. It seems that some kids frame their experience of life on the street as being the gateway to freedom, the ultimate in being real, authentic, alive. Hetherington (1998) suggests that the experience of kids who travel represents "...more than just a youth culture; in some ways they are more like a new social movement or form of cultural politics with an interest in issues such as those associated with the environment, communal and alternative living and lifestyles, anti-road protests, and access and rights to common land" (329). Although I want to account for the fact that street kids may present with issues differentiated from those of youth who travel in the countryside (i.e., kids who are kicked out of home versus kids who are expressly choosing an alternative lifestyle), as Hetherington (1998) proposes, perhaps there is something to be said for the significance of street kids acknowledging the positive consequences of their street life experiences.

But despite whatever reconfigurations we might calibrate in coming to understand street life for kids, "the good" is accompanied by "the bad and the ugly." A totally romantic view of street life can be misread in its excessive glamorization (Lees, 1998), and is eschewed by the kids with whom I spoke as mythology or urban lore. Although street kids seemed to be able to appreciate what is good, and true, and real about life on the street and their experiences therein, and although they are articulate about how their experiences on the street have taught them important life lessons, they negate the highly romanticized version of what it is like to be a street kid as hype and stereotype.

Many of the conversations I had with street kids explored differing ideologies on what street life is. The good, represented above, shows how kids can frame their experiences of the street in a positive light. The bad, represented a little further on, will illustrate how kids simultaneously understand their lives as awful. But there is an additional space that highlights the two, that throws both into light in terms of how the myths of the street are manifest and how certain kids act on that myth by both being attracted to the street and making their way there.

One of the most prevalent issues which emerged in my conversations with street kids was about a particular group of kids who come to the street for adventure. Classified as "part-time" versus "real" street kids, "twinkies" are named by the kids with whom I spoke as kids who think it's cool to hang out downtown, who live on the street part-time, or who have temporarily run away from home (as opposed to being kicked out). Jayne said this about twinkies:

> Sure, when you start living on the street, it's all fun and games, but it's not. All the twinkies in the summertime, "Yeah I'm going to the streets," and as soon as winter hits, they're gone. It's not fun, this life. Like there's good times, good people, you meet good good friends, you know who your friends really are, but it's not a life to have. (Jayne, 11/10/98)

So something attracts twinkies to the street, maybe the mythology of freedom. Street kids seem to understand their experiences in relation to and in opposition to the twinkies. There seems to be something "cool" about being on the street, and I'm trying to figure out what the attraction is. Mike talks about the street's image as that which attracts twinkies.

> I guess it's just the image. I guess it's just, being a street kid; I don't know, they think it's cool. And they don't see the bad side of it...they don't see us not eating for two days and not finding a place to sleep and having to shiver every night because they just see us when we're out-and-about downtown walking around and they look at us and "Wow, that guy is cool." They're lured into the life because for them it looks like a 24-hour slumber party because just all your friends are there and there are no rules and it's just a big party. My friend said that's what she first thought it was like and then after she started hanging around with all of us, she realized that it's not like that at all. (Mike, 10/08/98)

Illustrative of the confusion and ambiguity that exists in youth culture with respect to what the street might and mightn't be, there seems to be a significant draw to the street for kids living on the periphery of the mainstream, perpetuated perhaps by a romantic, hippie-like perception of what the street is and what it might offer. Whatever the case, this middle space of street lore helps to frame how kids understand their experiences of the street. They are clear about not being twinkies themselves and chastise twinkies for taking up their space. "The ones [twinkies] that just come and panhandle and hang out downtown because they think it's fun, them I'd like to smack" (Nicole, 09/02/98). And so more light is shed on how kids are making sense of their lives on the street. It is not alright to think that life on the street is fun and games, and that's why twinkies are rejected by entrenched street kids. Their lives are hard, and it seems that they want to make sure I know it.

Grub was unsure about talking to me. He watched me for several months, engaging in casual conversations with me before deciding to trust me with his story, to sit with me and share his experience. He is a young man with eyes that look like they've seen too much. He's quiet and gentle. He offered a different point of view than that of the mainstream about being on the street and panhandling, a view that is also commonly heard in the voices of other street kids.

> I hate panning. I would rather not do it, but you know, sometimes I have no choice…Like when you're panning, it's embarrassing, it's humiliating, it's degrading because you're basically begging for other people's money that they worked for and they earned. And we're just sitting there asking for it. I don't really blame people for not respecting that at all. I know I don't. (11/02/98)

Other than a few passing references in the literature to panhandling (e.g., Hagan & McCarthy's [1997] discussion around youth underemployment and lack of viable economic routes for earning money on the street, or Ruddick's [1996] commentary on punks in Hollywood reverting to panhandling as an uncomfortable form of sustenance), there is virtually no discussion about this central street kid activity. But the fact that panhandling is such a common street kid enterprise beckons the question as to why so little is said about this experience. Maybe it's too ugly to name; maybe we simply don't want to engage it; maybe we can't bear to face the destitution that we abide in the lives of our children.

Grub tells us clearly that within the purview of mainstream values (i.e., earning money) he is a societal parasite and that he can't even respect himself. Crowchild described the ruthlessness of the street for kids this way:

> [W]e are trash to them [referring to the mainstream]. We are nothing. We are something that they hope will die soon so they don't have to step over us when we are sleeping in a park because we have nowhere else to go. You know someone needs to get out of the way. Like if a street kid gets shot, nobody hears about it. No one will hear anything about it. It'll just be put on to another piece of paper as some John Doe. That's it. No grave. Maybe a grave but there will be no name on it. They will have no ceremony or nothing. Just dead, you're gone, big deal. (Crowchild, 09/02/98)

When Grub says that he doesn't respect himself for panhandling, I wonder what kind of impact that has on him, in the short-term, for the long-term. When Crowchild acknowledges his complete insignificance as a street kid who wouldn't even merit a grave, what does that mean for him, for you, for me? Laura offers this about her experience of the street:

> It's scary. Like, I don't care what anybody says, you can't get used to living on the streets. You can't do it. A lot of people say, "Oh I'm used to it." You know. "There's no problems. I'm used to living on the streets." You can't get used to it. Your body—you can't get used to sleeping in different places every night, not knowing where your next meal is going to come from, not knowing if you are going to go to sleep and not wake up in the morning. Like you don't know if you are going to go to sleep and wake up and not have anything in the morning because someone took it all when you were sleeping. You don't know if you are going to freeze to death while you are sleeping or anything. You don't know if you are going to be walking down the street and someone is going to jump you and rape you, or jump you and kill you or anything. You can't get used to those feelings. And you can't get used to the feeling of not having any family. And having to look at people, just walking down the street, and think that they think of you as street trash. And thinking of you as so much lower than them because they have money. Because they have a job and a house they can live in. They are so much better than you. But I don't know. Personally, I think that a lot of the people that I have met on the streets are the best people that I have met in my whole life. Like your money and your house and your way of life does not make you who you are. It doesn't. I think that a lot of people that I have met out here are the smartest group that I have ever met too. Because you have to be so smart when you live out here. You have to have the street smarts or you don't survive. That is just the way it goes. (Laura, 10/05/98)

From all that I had figured out about kids' lives on the street, I knew that panhandling could hardly be understood in a vacuum. For one thing, the mythology of the street was apparent in the youth culture beyond the kids who were homeless. For another, panhandling seemed to be a mainstay of street kids' experiences on the street. But what the twinkies illuminated about life on the street is that it is connected to the culture in which it happens even beyond the locality and specificity of asking people for money on a particular street in a particular city. According to what I had learned so far about this central street kid activity, this was the act that bridged the space between the mainstream and the homeless. Panhandling seemed to be the embodied expression of an "us" and a "them." But looking at what the kids said about panhandling, I realized that within this dichotomous trap, kids fibrillated in an endless flip-flop frenzy, trying to get a grip on where panhandling fits in for them and, further, where they fit in it. They seemed confused and conflicted about what this all means, what it says about society and, more importantly, what it says about them. Within their own interpretations of how the street is both understood as good and bad, there was vacillation as great and as furious as the tide of an angry sea continually lapping the shores, changing at every minute, re-constituting itself and reinventing itself every time around. One view, momentarily uttered—with confidence and strength, pride and hope—is that street life is about respect and community, about freedom, fun, and love. Yet almost in the same breath street life is conceived of as an endless series of painful experiences infused with fear and shame, insecurity and boredom, anger, hate, and regret. And still, there are incalculable spaces in between which make up the gamut of street life experience. There isn't a singular, static view that encapsulates the totality of the panhandling life. Panhandling is a dynamic, shifting, and changing enterprise that continually affords new meanings to kids about their lives and is invested with power relationships that mitigate the act of asking others for money. I learned that even within one conversation street kids can sway through the complexity of their lives like a pendulum suspended far above their reach. The breadth of their narratives exposed me to the multiple interpretations they made of their panhandling experiences. Journeying through what their experiences were like afforded me the opportunity to also hear about how panhandling in place exemplifies their relationships with the mainstream.

Sticks and Stones May Break My Bones
But Ignoring Me Is Killing Me

The chasm between the counted and the discounted occupied a central focus for the kids on the street. "Excuse me sir, spare some change so we can get home? Thank you." Neil is being ignored. "…[H]ave a nice night. Spare some change, sir, to help me get home?" Someone else walks by. "I hate it when they ignore us. I don't mind being told 'no,' but just acknowledge that we're here" (Neil, 08/14/98). "Yeah," Bobby agrees, "just acknowledgment makes you feel better" (08/14/98). Acknowledgment seems like a fairly modest expectation to have but is nevertheless lacking in the accounts that street kids offer about their lives. Zena says, "I hate it when people ignore me. When people say 'no,' I say, 'at least you can acknowledge my existence'" (08/24/98). "If I ask you something," Crowchild pleads, "even if I'm panhandling or squeegeeing, don't pretend I'm a brick wall. Don't pretend that I am just not there, or someone not worth talking to" (09/02/98). I hear a litany of voices screaming out, "Count us, see us, hear us, notice." Mike says:

> What I find really funny is that, okay, all these people in these cars passing by this window right now, and the people walking on the street and everything, are living in a completely different world than I am, and my friends are. It's really funny, because it's two completely separate worlds, but it just takes place in the same scenery, you know. The things that I do every day and the things they do every day and the things we experience are just so different that it's really hard to even believe that they're taking place in the same city. I don't think a lot of people realize that. They just don't realize that the life we live isn't anything like theirs, nothing at all. It's just like two different plays going on in the same stage. (Mike, 10/08/98)

Every time I hear them talk about being ignored, I recoil. Every time they name it, I feel guilty for being an adult, for being part of the procession of people trying to get them "in line" or to fit in, for being part of the "them" that are disrespectful of youth. Gwen Danzig and I were talking. I was taping my conversation with him and we were sitting on a pedestrian mall. He was reading aloud from an anarchist pamphlet and was talking with me about democracy and freedom, about oppression and economics; he was talking to me about being a street kid and how these concepts are continually interrelating with his life as a homeless kid. I was impressed by the assessment he proffered about his experiences on the street, and more, of his connections between those experiences and the greater social order around him. I asked if I could photocopy the pamphlet so that I could read it. He said "sure."

The ensuing moments on the street dumbfounded me. He set about asking passersby where we might be able to find a photocopy machine. Always beginning with "Excuse me, Ma'am" or "Excuse me, Sir," Gwen approached person after person, but nobody stopped. He was polite, gentle, calm, non-threatening, but that didn't seem to matter. He was relegated to the underclass, his presence a nuisance; he seemed invisible. I sat quietly beside him amazed and enraged at the parade of people ignoring this young man. Hello?! Anybody out there? Is this the kind of treatment that we deem helpful to the kids living on the street? And beyond helpful, how about respectful?

I had spent only two months on the street but it was enough to kick-start a sequence of questioning that asked how adults are interconnected with kids on the street. I could only imagine that these passersby were among the many nameless adults in the mainstream who apparently found it no matter that kids were sitting on the streets asking for change. In my own constructions, in my own attempt to untangle what I was seeing on the street, I imagined that these were adults who had told themselves a million stories about how these kids got there, had convinced themselves about who these kids are and what they're really doing, and had assured themselves that they were not any part of the problem. Perhaps my judgments were harsh, unfair, self-righteous, too simple. Whatever the case, I knew that there was something volatile, visceral, frenetic about how the adults in the mainstream connected and disconnected with street kids.

Gwen told me that being ignored is common. After a minute or two, I agreed to find a copy place on my own, if for no other reason than to put an end to him being ignored—it was regular street fare for him, but I couldn't stand it. He seemed glad to have had the opportunity to show me, to prove to me how he is positioned as a pariah in the landscape of the street. My mouth hung open in surprise. I wondered if I had ever treated kids on the street this way; I wanted to die if I had. This moment taught me that ignoring street kids is perhaps the most hurtful of all the experiences of the street. I can't help but surmise that the constant reminder of their nothingness will always speak to them about who they are and who they have been.

Ignoring kids seemed to hurl them into precarious spaces where their souls and selves could get beaten and bruised, where they were backed into the confined corners that are the sites for kids' struggles on the street. I could not dismiss the fact that kids were talking to me about being ignored and that they were implicating us in the process, whether through sins of omission or commission, whether intended or not. Offering compelling evidence about how they are mistreated and dismissed by the mainstream, by the passersby with whom they have daily contact, by adults who might otherwise be their allies, their help, their connection, street kids showed me something about the street scene. They try to resist being discounted and attempt to mark their territory by laying claim to their dignity despite the perpetual disdain flowing their way. "I'm used to people hating me just because I'm there," Mike states casually, as if it doesn't really bother him, as if he is above it—not letting the hate seep into his armor, as if it's nothing new (10/05/98). He drags on his cigarette and takes a swig of coffee as proof of his indifference. Admittedly his appointed place in our societal hierarchy offends him, and he deems it to be unjust. Later he explains:

> I hate putting myself in an inferior position because I'm not. I mean, I'm the same as everyone else. But when you put yourself on the street, like sitting down you know, "Spare some change, Sir, spare some change, Ma'am." These are people that, they've done nothing to deserve my respect and they're put in a position where they can treat me like total garbage just because I'm asking, just because they know they have that power. (Mike, 10/08/98)

Mike is particularly eloquent about his station in life. He explains how power, money, privilege, and respect are all intertwined in the silent contracts of Western values, values that position him in the periphery, make him invisible, make him disappear. But Mike seems to see something in it. He understands that his own disenfranchisement is a result of a society that conflates economic status with social status. He claims that today's respect has more to do with money and power than it does with goodness, or honor, or decency. It smacks of the truth when he says it, and it stings inside me when I hear it. I can't help thinking that he's right. Like a prophet pronouncing the clan's sinful idolatry, Mike strips us bare and lays it out unabashedly.

> [T]he thing that I find really funny is that people, when they look at me, they think that I'm this horrible demon and stuff like that, but if they sat down and talked to me for two minutes, they would find out that I'm not so bad. (Mike, 10/08/98)

But the sad reality is that for the dislocated and the excommunicated there are few opportunities to connect with others in the mainstream in positive ways. Finding out who they "really" are certainly does not seem to be a priority for most of the folks who walk by. Kids feel like they have been ousted and dismissed. They are ignored and feel like they've been forgotten. These circumstances contribute to their identities as homeless, roofless, moneyless street dwellers who are neither wanted nor tolerated, kids who are, nonetheless, struggling to make meaning of their lives in the contested spaces of the street.

The Street Is Who I Am

The embodied experience of being a street kid involves actually being situated in the geography of the street and being marginalized by the constraints and obstacles imbedded in the physicality of the street scene per se. But the street marginalizes its occupants beyond the bodily manifestation of homelessness. The street is also where kids seem to get categorized and identified, characterized and oppressed, based upon the iconography of the spaces that they occupy. Ruddick (1996) suggests that "…people are not simply marginalized in space but also through space [and therefore], it is also through space that they attempt to challenge this process and construct for themselves different identities" (49). Hanging on to whatever is good, and authentic, and valuable about their experiences of being homeless, and struggling with what is bad, and hurtful and scary about life on the street, street kids try to resist succumbing to the negative perceptions of self that could be so easily donned. Many kids speak to the relationships that develop on the street as a source of comfort, comradery, and pride in combatting what assails them from outside. Others identify freedom as that which represents their sense of personhood. Whatever the case, street kids say that they've learned invaluable lessons about themselves and others because of their experiences on the street and can tell you precisely what those lessons have been for them.

"[B]eing on the street messes up your head, y'know, like you can take the rat out of the street but you can't take the street out of the rat" (Laura, 10/5/98). Laura fears that she will always feel like a street kid, that the street has become part of her. She talks about how street life is infused in her sense of self, mingled together in who she is and was, who she might be, or can be, or would like to be, unified like the fluid steeping of black tea into the boiling water that surrounds it. She acknowledges that the street affects her beyond what she feels she can control.

Not feeling, or believing in, or recognizing, or being able to access her own sense of agency, Laura seems to believe that the street will always be a part of her. And so it goes that life on the street cultivates identities, good, bad, and otherwise. It gives rise to kids coming to know themselves and their world by understanding their place in it. Jayne offers this about the opportunities afforded to her because of her experience as a street kid:

> I don't know, like when you're living on the streets, I think you find yourself more than you would anywhere else. You know who you are, and you find out who you are, and what's important to you, and what's not, and what you can live with, and what you can live without. You learn a lot about, like, people and yourself, a lot. (Jayne, 11/10/98)

Part of that learning seems to be about incorporating street experiences into self-understandings. Mike suggests that being a street kid has become an indelible part of his identity, a part of himself that doesn't quit, that doesn't go away, that sits and settles and ossifies in the marrow of his bones. He says:

> I mean like it's become such a mainstay in my head, you know, and that's where I think when I get an apartment and stuff like that, I'm still going to look at myself as homeless because for, you know, like the past while, I've been, you know, that's what I've been, homeless. It's just like, people when they think of me, they're like, "Oh, he's homeless." (Mike, 10/08/98)

And so Mike's self-perception is enveloped in what others have made of him. His identity as a street kid, as a panhandler, is consolidated in his homelessness. What does that mean for him as he faces his future? How will his experience of street life impact his life after the street? Is there an "after the street" for the self that grows up there, or develops there, or awakens there to the mammoth issues of power and privilege, justice and social order? Of course the answers to these questions are bound up in futures that none of us can prescribe, or detect, or foresee. But hearing what kids had to say about themselves was not confined to the boundaries of themselves. The confluence of conditions that arise such that kids come to assign meaning to their lives on the street appears to be inevitably and inextricably tied up in the corporeal interactions between themselves and others.

> I don't know. It's kind of like a black hole. Once you get on the streets, you're used to a routine. You're used to living one sort of way, and you get so used to, you know, sleeping in the bushes or sleeping under bridges and stuff like that, and it's hard to get out of that. Like people, like whenever I've gotten off the streets and gotten into an apartment, my very first instinct is always to get right back, like not get on the streets but it's always to still be around all the time but just go home at night and still try to do the same things that I always did. It's hard because you get so used to it, and it's drilled into your head every day that you're homeless, by everybody. Like there's not one day that goes by that people don't call me a bum, that people don't call me dirty street trash. I mean, even the cops call me a dirty street rat, you know, and there's never once that I can forget that I'm homeless and just be a person, you know. (Mike, 10/08/98)

Longing to be a person, to be counted, to be respected beyond his lowly status, Mike explains how the street has become home. Within the company of his street contemporaries, Mike is more at peace, less judged, a little less alienated, better understood—no doubt a welcome respite from what faces him in the regularity of his life as a panhandling street kid. "[A]fter a while it starts to grow on you and you start to cope with it and so it doesn't seem as bad, and then you just don't really have any desire to get off," Grub explains to me. "[Y]ou don't really make street life; street life makes you, and you gotta just kinda live around it sort of thing, live in it" (Grub, 11/02/98). But living in it can be heavy, and the price of one's self can be dear.

I just don't want to start accepting some of the bad things that go on. Before I used to look at things like smoking crack and prostitution as being really, really bad, that I would never, ever do it, but now, I kinda think that some things are okay. I don't see why that has changed. And I still hope that I'm not going to do them, but I look at them differently now and I still want to, like I used to not hang around with anybody who worked the stroll, at all, I didn't associate with them, I didn't talk to them. Now I understand where they're coming from better and it kind of scares me because if I was ever in the same situation, I'm hoping that I wouldn't do the same thing, but you never know. My beliefs are changing the longer I'm out here. More and more things are becoming okay to do. It just doesn't seem right because I know that, like right now, when I look out on society, I see people, okay, suits. People who wear suits, they think of all these things as wrong and I used to think of all those things as wrong too, but now I do them. I don't know why that's changed and I don't want it to change anymore because it's just getting worse and worse. It's like [my values], they're slipping. (Nicole, 09/02/98)

I hear how street life accosts Nicole's sense of order. Unclear about what is happening to her, Nicole admits that she is changing.[10] Values and beliefs, morals and selves, seem to be up for grabs in the precarious spaces of street life for kids. One's location, physical and/or representational,

---

[10] Nicole's comments with regard to how her values are changing over time on the street present an interesting invitation to explore the conditions in which that can happen. In the street kid literature, as well as in criminology literature, the criminogenic situation has been offered to help explain the nature and impetus for criminal activity perpetrated on the street by youth. Hagan and McCarthy (1997) suggest that it is street life itself which fosters increased criminal behavior because of the particular conditions of the street (e.g., lack of resources, hunger, etc.). They state that whereas much of the current literature on youth crime is focused on the characteristics of the individuals committing the crimes, the focus should be re-targeted to account for the places and spaces in which these crimes are committed, and take into account the contexts from which these kids come. This is called the criminogenic situation and the social capital theory—acknowledging that the environment of the kid and place of the crimes are the problem (i.e., ontogenic as well as sociogenic influences). I believe that Hagan and McCarthy (1997) did not go far enough in exploring how the street erodes street kids' senses of self, conceptions of values, and codes of morality, because their investigations focused on crime. As a result of what I learned about panhandling, about being ignored, and about street kids' feelings of rejection from the mainstream, I propose that Nicole's "slipping values" are at least in part a consequence of her exposure to the brutality of how she is named and identified on the street as "scum," how she is pushed further into the street scene by the assaulting mainstream. Perhaps her changing identity is therefore a response to oppression and marginalization rather than a fault of her character. Exposed to the constant battles for dignity, for identity, for respect, Nicole's values slowly erode into the subjugated spaces of the street, and her embodied experience as a street kid intensifies.

forms social identities (Pile & Thrift, 1995; Ruddick, 1996, 1998). And so it is that the young souls who appropriate the spaces of the street to make it their home confront a myriad of conflicting stories about who they are and the kind of life that they are leading in their identities as street kids.

It seemed to me that the realities of the street were molding and forming its inhabitants beyond their will. I came to see that sometimes identities could get muddled along the path, could get hijacked before they have a chance to escape whatever damage might be caused by extended exposure to being a kid on the street. But let me clarify what exposure I'm referring to and what I'm calling up. It isn't the physical hardship the kids face on the street in the course of their lives there, but rather the constant rejection and repulsion the kids say is assailing them from the mainstream. What would the experiences of the street be like if the views of non-homeless people were mostly compassionate? How would street kids feel if the public with whom they interacted treated them with respect and with dignity? What would it be like if passersby understood their circumstances a little better, and more, even accepted some responsibility for their plight? How would we conceive of street kids if the boundaries between us were blurred and the dichotomies that keep us comfortably separated suddenly disappeared?

Contorting to accommodate the conflicting messages of who they are and what they represent, street kids try to muddle through, try to make meaning of who they are, try to resist derisive assessments, straddling the in-betweens of liberation and occupation, and cast for themselves spaces in which subversive subjectivities resist being nullified, and vilified, and objectified. Coming to know themselves as the "street rats" they've been named, recognizing how things shift under the heavy artillery of mainstream scorn, and finding themselves marginalized on all fronts, kids can't help but capitulate to the identities that have been inscribed upon them and also those they've inscribed on themselves. Born of their experiences of the street, kids' identities hover in the confused spaces between being agents of their own lives and slaves to the social orders and mainstream views that oppress them. By street kids being positioned on the outside, by being forced to the edges, street kids are able to take a discriminating look in at us. In strengthening their resolve that in fact they are not what the mainstream makes of them, contesting the discourses that operate upon them, asserting their identities beyond the equation of "street scum," street kids have a unique opportunity to evaluate their lives in contrast to our own. Their identities are surely contested, but it is they who want to make sure that what they are about has not been settled by the mainstream in perpetuity.

Chapter Four

The Chaos of Connections

In Chapter Three the embodied nature of panhandling was identified and explored as a central physical and symbolic experience through which kids struggle to understand and interpret their lives on the street. Panhandling was probed for how it is positioned and positions kids in the interpretations of their experiences of the street, for its centrality in the lives of street kids, and for its impact in street kids' cultivating, adopting, and/or contesting their identities as marginalized and disenfranchised persons. Focussing on the conflicted locale where street kids eke out meanings while subsisting in the margins, Chapter Three contemplates how confused identities are painfully forged through the narrow crevices that exist for kids in the troubled and contested spaces of the street.

The embodied experience of being a street kid is connected to the mainstream through an exploration of the difficult relationships that exist in the in-between spaces of the street, for example, through street kids' experiences of being ignored. By visiting the complexities that inhabit this site for kids, both confusion and clarity emerge as central circumstances of their experiences. Street kids try to repel, resist, and reject negative images of who they are through their agency as street dwellers, either by naming their experience in terms of freedom, or by finding whatever is good about what happens to them on the street and using that to frame their experiences. Kids counter with their confessions and cast demarcations of their own, separating the "suits" or "corporate assholes" from themselves, and identifying pejorative mainstream assumptions as economically motivated power plays. Beginning to see how the experience of the street provides the contested space for kids' identities to be inscribed both by their interpretations as well as by the circumstances in which they live in the streetscape, we come to understand that the streetscape is a site where kids are gazed at, stared at, looked upon with all the contempt and condescension that festers in the in-between spaces that separate street kids from other, as other. We know that street kids are gazed at, but are they not gazers as well (Crouch, 1998)?

This chapter will examine the larger systems with which the streetself collides, to which the self is inextricably attached, and in which the self is shadowed. In addition to constructing and reflecting on their personal experiences of the street, street kids also spoke in tandem about the larger sociopolitical milieu in which they find themselves. This is what I will take up here. Looking at what the kids said about their experience of the street, we will expand our circle of interpretation to include the larger systems with which the kids' experiences intersect.

Deeply connected to their environs, and speaking from positions well beyond the borders of the mainstream, street kids explore the complicated spheres of social justice, political ideology, and economic doctrine in their tellings about their experience of the street. Pile and Thrift (1995) explain that "[t]he body becomes a point of capture, where dense meanings of power are animated, where cultural codes gain their apparent coherence and where the boundaries between the same and the other are installed and naturalized" (40). Their bodily presence on the street is similarly a site for capture.

Open Your Gutters and Close Your Eyes
and You Will Get a Big Surprise:
The Personal Is Political

[M]y friend and I, we always, we panhandle up on 17th, people always ignore us, like if we ask for change, like they don't even look at us. Usually the comeback I have is always, "Oh geez, I forgot, I'm invisible." The thing is, I'm not invisible. You can see me right now. But the thing is I'm invisible in their world. They don't want to look at me because they don't want to acknowledge me, because to acknowledge me is to acknowledge the fact that there is a homeless problem and to acknowledge the fact that I need help and I need food and they can give it to me. (Mike, 10/08/98)

We may all feel like invisible strangers in the isolated spaces of the street. Still, I wondered what it must be like to be an explicit and repeated target of evasion, erasure, expulsion. For Mike, being invisible seems to have ramifications beyond how that must hurt him personally. He acknowledges the greater political climate in which he finds himself and calls it up to account for the actions of the people with whom he interacts as a panhandler. To illustrate his point, Mike uses the following as an example of how much his presence in the public sphere is reviled.

> I sleep under a bridge and on the other side of the bridge is a path that joggers and people on their bikes, they go by every morning and stuff, and there's a lot of people that sleep under this bridge, you know. We have mattresses and stuff like that, and the City is trying to clean it out right now. They're trying to get all of us away from there because they've had complaints that we're there. And I think it's really funny because I know who those complaints are from, it's from the morning joggers and the people with their dogs, like, "Oh no, look at those dirty homeless people, I don't like that, I don't like to see that on my morning jog, can you do something about that?" And I was joking with my friend last night, I was just saying you know, they're just going to dig big holes for us and it's going to be like, "Here this is your hole, don't come out, make sure we can't see you," and they'll put our name on each one of them. It's just, people don't want us to exist. (Mike, 10/08/98)

Mike's remarks seem to exemplify both his personal experience of being ignored and ostracized as a homeless kid, as well as his threatened citizenship. His minimal use of public space puts him at risk for politically sanctioned removal and expulsion. Giroux (1996) suggests that "the conditions and problems of contemporary youth will have to be engaged through a willingness to interrogate the world of public politics" (53), and so it is that Mike's experience with the joggers, and the park, and the city impels us to do just that.

When Mike told me that story, shared with me his interpretations of the municipal government's attempt to remove him from the landscape, when Mike cogently pieced together the larger puzzle of public disdain with which he lives daily, I wanted to know more about how street kids represent their personal stories in their representations of space and marginalization on the street. By stating that his sleeping under a bridge was causing some civil unrest, I understood that street kids' experiences were connected to ever-widening systems of our civil, social, political, and economic arrangements. Fragments of stories I'd heard before began to make sense to me as I learned more and more about the politically, socially, and economically textured experiences of street kids' lives. The complex and intricate tapestry of kids' street life felt incomplete. I understood something about kids' experience panhandling on the street but was exploring how these experiences were connected to other things. Threads of that tapestry began to surface. I started to think about adjoining these threads into a greater story, a story that would encompass more of the intricacies intertwined in the totality of street life, our living together, and all the troubledness in between.

I harkened back to trails, to clues, to moments in my conversations with street kids and before that caught my attention. The flood of bits and morsels relating to street kids' experiences on the street had begun long ago, but it was now that the momentum started to accelerate. The Rolex watch, cleaning up garbage, the naming of corporate versus other adults, the separation of class and status, my previous experience with the agency and with the woman who spoke to me about setting up my research, the feelings I had about technology and the youth-trade industry, all began to converge into a massive mental file crowded with fragments and pieces that kept calling into question the greater values that undergird the ways in which we live together. The file was rapidly filling and I was feeling its weightiness.

I began to hear how street kids act as resisters or non-compliers in the political, economic, and social agendas of dominant culture ideologies, and how this is so much a part of their experiences of the street, not to mention a part of the discursively constituted identities they carve out for themselves on the street. Manifest in their situatedness on the street, homeless kids seemed to have ample opportunity to comment, reflect, and critique the predominant cultural viewpoints which set them apart from the mainstream. Shaped by the personal but infused with the political and economic, street kids' narratives stepped into and retreated from ideological and philosophical musings. In understanding that dominant ideologies and policies are ultimately designed to remove them, it seemed that many street kids were taking up the enormity of evaluating the human condition as they saw and experienced it. I puzzled over how I was going to set their stories in and against the Western values that they were invoking in order to bring to bear their profound observations, but I knew that however I did, the connections that street kids made about their lives were critical to address and expose.

Mike's accounts stuck in my head for a long while. Dig a hole for me, make me invisible, get rid of me, cast me out, ignore me, shun me, leave me, kill me. What could that mean for Mike? What does that mean for us? Make him invisible? Why? Maybe we're afraid.

"Evicted from the public as well as the private spaces of what is fast becoming a downtown bourgeois playground" (Smith, 1996, 28), street kids are finding themselves increasingly spaceless in addition to homeless. They seem keenly aware of the political machinery that is focused on removing them from the landscape and are hostile to the takeover. This political fight is complicated. The battle is waged in the embodied geography of the street and in the discourses of power, money, and privilege which extend beyond the locality of the street. It seems clear to me after connecting the personal accounts of street kids to the political ramifications thereof that these issues need to be a part of any understanding of the spaces that kids inhabit on the street. "Negative images of youth and the increased privatization of public space both result in public policies that seek to remove young people from public spaces, delimit their geography and enforce their invisibility" (Breitbart, 1998, 307). The circle widens even further.

Personal, Political, and Planetary

Even all those months ago I puzzled over how I could connect all the parts of this story to a greater whole. Somehow I thought that ecology could speak directly to how we might begin to approach the task of understanding other people's lives as we come to understand our own, and discover something about our immutable connections to each other and to the earth. Who am I to take on such a task, I heard myself asking? Trained as an academic, I wanted to find a framework into which I could place all the aspects of street kids' experiences. Nice, neat, easy. Why are connections so important? I heard myself nagging. I was ill-prepared for the vastness of the topic and/or my thinking about the topic. Serves me right, I heard myself scolding. Not expecting the narratives of street kids to extend into the political, social, psychological, spiritual, and economic realms of living nearly to the extent that they did, I was catapulted into chaos—the chaos of the street and the chaos of connections.

I had criticized the literature on street kids for compartmentalizing, for severing the minutiae of street kids' experiences into barely recognizable bits, castrating the whole for the sake of the parts. I wanted to avoid making the same mistake. So what did I expect? I heard myself questioning. I had imagined that the data would present as more particular in terms of the functionings of street life. But in their stead the entirety of street kids' lives came barreling at me—full speed—replete with every complexity and every tendril extended into every topic, idea, and factor. No shit, Sherlock, I heard myself laughing.

Reading Capra (1996) crystalized an idea that had been formless, and nameless, and ethereal for me as I worked in, and struggled through, my experiences on the street with kids. Perhaps both a priori and subsequent forays into systemic thinking led me here, led me to a place where connections converse with the complexities of the human condition.[11] *Capra speaks about the deep ecology movement in terms of understanding the world as a series of interrelated, interdependent organisms—systems that function together, affect each other, and are essentially and inevitably connected. Aha! I felt myself finding my way. Deep ecology "sees the world not as a collection of isolated objects, but as a network of phenomena that are fundamentally interconnected and interdependent. Deep ecology recognizes the intrinsic value of all living beings and views humans as just one particular strand in the web of life" (Capra, 1996, 7). It was here that part of my answer lay and here that the tributary to an ever-evolving and widening circle of inquiry was irreversibly thrust open.*

My inquiry into deep ecology quickly led to me to imagine what a concept like "deep psychology" might encompass. I needed to find a

---

[11] Systemic thinking in psychology and other fields is well established. I am familiar with Bowler's (1981) General Systems Thinking, and more specifically with the systemic philosophies and approaches of the constructivist psychotherapies (e.g., Becvar & Becvar, 1994; Capra, 1982, 1996; Gergen, 1994; Guidano, 1995a, 1995b; Lyddon, 1995 ; Mahoney 1988a, 1988b, 1995; Neimeyer & Mahoney, 1995).

psychology that could speak to, and account for, the breadth of street kids'
experiences, including and especially their political philosophizing as part
of how they understand themselves and their world. I needed a new
language to talk about, and through, what the kids were teaching me about
the street as well as what I was piecing together through my experiences
there.

I understood that this inquiry needed to account for the multiply
constituted experience of street kids and the totality of their lives as they
explained how they are deflected from and rejected by mainstream
institutions. I knew this work needed to reflect the connectedness of the
various systems in the production and maintenance of the street kid
phenomenon, especially as the kids delivered up those connections in our
conversations. I tentatively envisioned what a deep psychology could be
with regard to incorporating economics, politics, religion, and so forth into
an applied and down-to-earth understanding of lived experiences. I
imagined that a "deep psychology could account for and acknowledge the
intricate interconnectedness and interdependence of a dynamic
constellation of values, beliefs, actions, and perceptions which are
imbedded in the psyches of people and institutions, this psychology could
be ecologically and ethologically based" (Me, 09/03/98). I searched for
such a thing in the annals of psychological theory and found a few
interesting leads. Ecopsychology and environmental psychology offered
their support in promoting a holistic and comprehensive perspective on
human nature as part of, and not superior to, living systems and our planet
(see, for example, Roszak, Gomes, & Kanner, 1995). That seemed to work
but was focused primarily on environmental and biological aspects of life,
well-being, and sustainablity. Although my foray into that school of thought
was fruitful and did encompass parts of what I deemed to be essential
aspects of any philosophy of psychology or therapy, I searched further to
see if I could find a critical school of psychological thought that would, on
the one hand, speak to politics, economics, and power, and on the other
hand, open up a space for self-reflection and critique.

From deep ecology to ecopsychology and environmental psychology,
I finally got to critical psychology and breathed a sigh of relief. Although
the field is small and is partly an offshoot of social psychology, critical
psychology nevertheless begins to acknowledge political, economic, and

social facets of the human web of life, inevitably integrated in our planetary situatedness. Also, the critical psychology movement focuses much of its attention on psychology's participation and culpability in maintaining, strengthening, and reifying the status quo (see, for example, Fox & Prilleltensky, 1997; Ibáñez & Íñiguez, 1997; Prilleltensky, 1994; Sullivan, 1990). This seemed to be the burgeoning field of psychology that would extend to me the freedom that I needed to thoughtfully, carefully, and holistically inquire into the lives of street kids.

I thought awhile about why I was searching for a psychology that could save me. I had hermeneutics as a guiding approach to research in addition to being a philosophy that resonated with the way I think, feel, and take up the world. I wasn't wanting to become an expert in theory; in fact I believed theory had been part of how psychology maintained its distance from the realms of politics and economics in the first place. But, on the other hand, I also recognized that psychology was absent from the kinds of discussions about street kids that I wanted to have. Although my ecological perspective of street kids' lives made perfect sense to me (i.e., talking about politics, economics, values, social order, religion, power, environmental issues, etc.), I acknowledged my less-powered position as a neophyte in the academic world and hoped for back-up in support of my perspective from a friend in psychology. That said, I also felt deeply saddened and ashamed about needing, or wanting, or searching for legitimization in theoretical frameworks. Theory? Theory can become an abstraction a few too many steps away from the lived world as I was living it with the kids on the street. Do disciplinary paradigms lead us, as psychologists, educators, cultural theorists, academicians, and adults, to numb ourselves clear of what is happening in our relationships with ourselves, each other, our kids, our institutions, our political and economic climates, our ideologies, and our planet? As with everything else in this inquiry, I accepted having to live a while in the uncomfortable tensions that present themselves when the system that you're in is also the system that you instinctively resist.

Even though I felt a communion with a branch of psychology that might have been able to help me in some way, I also knew that searching for a meta-theory (i.e., one omnibus framework) to hide behind was the remnant of a positivist ghost trying to frighten me away from the "original complexities" and the messiness of life (Caputo, 1987; Smith, 1994). I put the search aside and committed to go back to it at a later time, committing to work toward initiating a shift in the way that psychology might take up an issue like street kids. In part, I hoped that this book might be a first small step toward that end. I stuck my nose back into my data, reacquainted myself with the hermeneutics that certainly afforded me and my interpretations the freedom to explore the complexity of connections, tensions, and problems, and continued trying to understand life on the street for kids.

The Disappearance of Public Space for Youth and The Body Politic

By listening to kids speak about the varying experiences of their lives as homeless people, I had arrived at questioning how street kids are positioned and impositioned in the greater systems of our social fabric. For example, Mike's story about the park was one of a number of tales that street kids told me with regard to the alleged effort to get rid of them. I began questioning how public space intersected in the lives of street kids and heard a lot about how kids feel they are positioned on the street. The kids' vacillating feelings about their street experiences extended into how they spoke about their identities as street kids, identities that were formed in part through the conditions of the street. In understanding the street to be simultaneously the site for resistance, exclusion, negotiation, contestation, and oppression (Baron, 1989; Carlen, 1996; Cresswell, 1998; Lees, 1998; Ruddick, 1996, 1998), I heard a lot about how kids make meaning and interpret their positions on the street. Street kids knew that the players on the street were not equally invested with power to claim their places and spaces. As Gwen Danzig remarked:

> We're supposed to have rights and freedoms. And we get out on the street and it seems that most of your rights and freedoms are stripped from you. I don't know, it's weird. In Canada there is no place you are legally allowed to sleep outside except for a road that has both ends blocked off, [and that's only] because it hasn't been written up yet. (Gwen Danzig, 08/25/98)

During my first formal interview on the street, I was told about, and invited to, another popular street kid hangout. Neil offered to take me, and introduce me, and show me the ropes . But I felt shy, and intimidated, and reluctant to go stomping through their places without first considering what that would mean for me and for them. In any case, some three weeks after my T-shirt had been spotted and I was regularly connecting with kids on the pedestrian mall, I did go over to this alternative street kid space. Neil, acting as my ambassador, welcomed me when I got there.

The locale itself was a small urban park in front of a convenience store, set on a busy street which housed many of the city's bars and popular dancing spots. It was a good place for panning, I was told. This urban park measured about thirty feet in length and roughly eight feet in width and was bordered by shrubs all around, encasing it in its own space. Inside there were benches and city garbage cans. Many of the benches were broken. One of the long sides of this space bordered the busy street; the other bordered the parking lot adjacent to the strip mall that housed the convenience store. It wasn't much of a real park, but enough of a place that kids could appropriate it as their own. The bushes around the rectangular space stood about five feet tall, and on the side of the parking lot there was a manicured entryway through the bushes into the space.

I had mentioned to the kids previously that I felt a bit uncomfortable about going to "the avenue" with them and asked them how they felt about it. They assured me that my coming to this place was no big deal and told me that most kids would love to have an opportunity to tell their stories.

One of the first times I went to "the avenue," I remember standing outside the hedged park feeling like an intruder. Finally, one of the kids I knew saw me and asked me why I didn't come in. I felt like an idiot for answering that I hadn't been invited and wanted to respect their place and space despite the fact that the space was public. I felt so much like an invader, like an intruder, like an outcast. To my mind, this was the kids' home, and it felt awkward for me to waltz right in, unannounced, irrespective of their wills and wants, just because I wanted to meet them, and know them, and listen to them, and write about them.

In reflections and discussions about how I felt as a researcher, person, and citizen with regards to kids making space and being alien in it, I was reminded that most of the adults with whom these kids connect would probably not hesitate to intrude. I thought that perhaps because I was querying the experiences of the street for kids and all their meanings, I was more inclined to examine how space was being appropriated by them and also by the mainstream. Also, it was pointed out to me that even though street kids aim to feel "at home" in public space, they're used to having that space invaded (T. Pirosok, personal communication, September, 1998). There was a tension between public and private spaces that I didn't quite understand. I couldn't put my finger on it but knew that it had something to do with the proposition that public space is sometimes synonymous with space for the invited or welcome, or perhaps something to do with my feeling that the privatization of public space is increasing, or that the legitimacy of public space at all is suspect if there is gross inequality among society's members (Daly, H.E., 1996; Daly, G., 1998; Korten, 1998). Within the ambiguous private/public space, I decided that, at least in terms of me being here, this public space was their space, and throughout my time on the street I was always mindful of my position as visitor, guest, and invited outsider. These were interesting issues to contemplate and I wondered how they fit into the bigger picture.

The kids made me comfortable, made me welcome, opened their space to me both literally and figuratively. It was alright for me to go there over time; I had their permission and that felt like the way it needed to be for me and I think also for them.

There's a big sign there now. You can't miss it. They've cut the bushes so that the space is no longer secluded from the street and parking lot. The bushes are about two feet high. I guess that space is no longer accepting street kids. The sign reads "PRIVATE PROPERTY."

Recently, the public spaces which kids inhabit are being contested and colonized away from them. It has been reported that "[m]ore than seventy American cities have criminalized activities associated with lack of shelter" (Daly, 1998, 121) and nearly a thousand cities "have inaugurate[d] or strengthene[d] curfews designed both to keep youth off the street and to police and criminalize their presence within urban space" (Giroux, 1996, 118). Redistributed or re-colonized by an economically advantaged populace, homeless kids are being squeezed out of the landscape. Literature on gentrification suggests that money, privilege, and power constitute the necessary ingredients for harvesting public spaces away from the less-powered, more-oppressed marginalized while simultaneously attempting to remove them from the public terrain (see, for example, Fyfe, 1998; Smith, 1996). Interestingly, the literature on street kids (in the domains of psychology, social work, and education, for example) is conspicuously quiet with regard to spacial considerations of the street and whatever interpretations would therefore arise from looking at space and place as contributors to the lives and conditions of the kids who live there.

Nevertheless, these issues do spring forth from the narratives of street kids as important signifiers of mainstream malevolence. The effort to effect these public evictions does not go unnoticed by the street kids, as is clearly evidenced above. Lees (1998) reminds us that "…the public space of the street is not pregiven, in either its form or its meaning. It is produced through contestation and social negotiation" (250). *But what negotiation can be initiated between street kids and the mainstream? Who make up the mainstream? Who are the power brokers and the gatekeepers? These questions seem ethereal, unanswerable, convoluted, complex. But I know that there is much to examine in understanding the multilayered aspects and facets of the streetspace and kids' experiences in it. I persevere.* Even if we were to submit that, in fact, negotiation or contestation was plausible, as Lees (1998) suggests, street kids are not perceived as stakeholders in the public space of the street and, therefore, warrant no real consideration, although they warranted some kind of negative consideration by inspiring the powers that be to cut down the bushes and put up a sign (J. Field, personal communication, July 1999). Furthermore, it seemed to me that kids' invitation to occupy public space was dependent on whether or not they were choosing to be street kids in the first place. If kids are making a choice about being homeless, then restricting their access or privilege and pushing them away from the street, perhaps toward home, could be viewed as a reasonable ethical and moral position to have. The error of this position is that for some kids (including the kids that I spoke to) street life is not a choice.[12] If it is conversely understood that kids are not making the choice to be on the street, then the moral imperative to address them, to acknowledge them, to help them, to connect with them, to not erase them, is so much the stronger.

> I think that it is just that a lot of people think that we put ourselves here. And it is like, we don't really have any reason to be on the street. I have gotten several, when I have been panning, someone will come up and go, "Go home, your parents love you." People don't understand how much that hurts when they say that. Because just knowing that they don't. Knowing that my mom doesn't want me there. And knowing that she hates me and wishes that she like, wishes she never had me and stuff. It really hurts when people say, "Go home your parents love you." I just can't stand it. And like, I think people just need something to look down on. To make themselves feel better. Like, to feel higher up and more mighty. And they just use us as an example. (Laura, 10/05/98)

But despite the underlying reasons for kids being on the street, and perhaps more importantly, notwithstanding the causes that lead kids to the street, the street is a hotly contested site in terms of who warrants what space or treatment under which circumstances. Vying for power and privilege on the street seems to become a matter of ensuring desirable or less desirable conditions, evidenced perhaps in the placard we spoke about earlier in Chapter Three (see Appendix III). A multitude of practices happen in the street, including, for example, leisure, gathering, and eating (Crouch, 1998). The vibrancy and viability of the streetspace is perceived as an indicator of economic health, social well-being, and political success in the urban imagination (Smith, 1996). Street kids readily understand and engage in the discourses of the streetscape, and ultimately make meaning about their sociopolitical lives by interpreting how space is defined or confined along with their viability in it. They do this in two ways. First, kids speak a lot about socioeconomic status as part of the way their

---

[12] Literature on the numbers of kids who are relegated to the street because they've been thrown out is virtually non-existent (Colby, 1990). One recent study suggested that only 6 percent of the kids stated that their "homelessness was desirable," i.e., a choice (Russell, 1998, 317). Moreover, definitional problems in the literature confound any real estimate with regard to who is a runner and who is a throwaway. Please see Appendix I for further explication on the causes and consequences of making the street home.

experiences are framed on the street. Economic status is somehow connected to the appropriation or entitlement of people in the streetscape. In other words, if you are part of "the system," you are welcome in the spaces of the street (T. Pirosok, personal communication, July 1999). Second, street kids recounted endless stories about police brutality as an exemplar of repressive and oppressive state-sanctioned spatial control. Accordingly, Daly (1998) suggests that "space is organized in political and legal terms to express ideas about civic virtue, to differentiate between those who are deserving and those who are regarded as transient, marginal, fugitive, or deviant" (124).

To this end, street kids' discursive treatment of economics, politics, and socioeconomic status was an integral component of what they shared with me about their experiences on the street. But there was also a third factor to laying out the political economy of the street to which the kids only spoke about marginally. As will be explicated, kids had articulated so much about their sociopolitical lives through their discussions of the embodied location in the streetscape as well as about economics, politics, and police, but they hadn't spoken a lot about the specific legal doctrines that were also operating per se. I was interested in how their experiences of disenfranchisement might be situated in a legal context, and so I investigated city ordinances, bylaws, and the general political climate which undergirds the discussion about kids and their lives on the street to further understand all that they were telling me.

City Ordinances as Public Erasing

Popular culture currently addresses, defines, and constructs the youth street scene as one which breeds crime, delinquency, danger, and chaos (see, for example, Carlen, 1996; Daly, 1998; Giroux, 1996; Hagan & McCarthy, 1997; Lees, 1998; Schissel, 1997). Can't you hear it? The newscaster is reporting that a homeless shelter is being erected in a certain district of the city, but there is a community association fighting to stop the project. Maybe we might pause and think about what that actually means in terms of human lives, in terms of people needing shelter, in terms of being benevolent and extending help where it is needed. Maybe we might consider what it means when we ponder where we would prefer to put the shelter or if we believe that a shelter should go up in the first place. The media is constantly screaming these exclusionary images at us, reinforcing the notion that homeless youth are dangerous, evil, out of control, agents of ruin and destruction, and criminals (Giroux, 1997; Schissel, 1997).

Casting them into them and us into us, we neatly, and nicely, and quietly separate our lives from those who make the street their home, and they seem to do the same to us. Like oil beading on water, integration between home dwellers and street dwellers is not what we are seeking to achieve in the public domain. And more still, the places and spaces that we want to visit, and roam, and be in, are increasingly becoming less hospitable to those who are marginalized, oppressed, or otherwise undesirable.

But it seems to me that there is more to the story than the fact that these spaces are becoming less welcoming to disenfranchised folk. When I started going downtown to speak with kids, I was apprehensive. It was an unknown space for me. I wasn't sure about my safety, and I didn't know about how I would be received for trying to cross the borders between those that make the street their home and those that don't.

Power and privilege are contested in the spaces of the street. There seems to be a struggle between at least two groups who are enacting upon and appropriating the streetscape in different ways. Both parties want to feel at home in the public spaces of the street, but it appears that there isn't enough space to accommodate the gamut of practices and meanings habituated in and by the street, literally and metaphorically. On one side, the street kids make these places and spaces their home, wanting or expecting that other members of society see and experience what they do. On the other side, mainstream folk use the street in their daily practices in a myriad of ways (Crouch, 1998), and may not be clued into, or aware of, what these spaces represent to others. Moreover, what if the increasing inhospitality of the street is seeping into the experiences of more than just street kids? What would it mean if the separations that we make, and the connections that we draw, cast us apart from each other in ways that are not easily reconcilable?

After having spent time on the street and after becoming comfortable and safe with the kids and in the space, I realized that through my acquaintance of the spaces and the people in the street, I gained a different appreciation for how fear and misunderstanding impact the separations named above (E. Mayers; T. Pirosok, personal communications, August 1999). But however I understood the complexity of the street in my musings and however I felt or feel about the street—no matter what my own feelings of alienation are or how they are exacerbated in the street, regardless of my fear or lack of understanding about others who share this space—I could not ignore that, because of my privilege, I was "free" to make place in that space. Street kids do not have that advantage. Whereas there is no blatant political or economic target on me, whereas there is no evident legal or political machinery trying to delimit my freedom on/in the streetscape, street kids seem to have bull's-eyes invisibly imprinted on their bodies.

Evidenced in city bylaws restricting kids' panhandling behavior, apparent in the languaging about who they are, why they are there, and what these kids are about, explicit in the moral panics around youth, and crime, and the street, homeless kids are being systematically evicted from the scene. Daly (1998) contends that "...the nature and complexity of homelessness can be more fully appreciated by examining the political economy of the state and the decisions made regarding resource distribution" (114). For the purposes of our discussion, the places and spaces of the street are the very resources that kids are competing for and in, and that kids are powerless to claim, even for small measures like shelter, or gathering, or panhandling. Access to these resources is being limited and constrained, controlled and monitored by governments, and influenced by corporate citizens who want to clear away the human debris that might inhibit consumers' unhampered access to their establishments. For example:

> The business community in Vancouver has voiced concern over the escalating problem with panhandlers. It [panhandling] creates an intimidating and unsightly atmosphere, negatively impacting on the quality of life of Vancouver's citizens while adversely affecting businesses and tourism in our city. (Administrative Report, 1998)

The Business Improvement Association (BIA) in Vancouver has long been trying to restrict panhandling activity. In the background documentation supporting the bylaw implementation, it states:

> Despite their efforts, new panhandlers arrive to fill the gaps while a core of chronic panhandlers remains. BIA's in the downtown business area have also supported a public education campaign encouraging people not to give change to panhandlers but to local charities instead. (Administrative Report, 1998)

Admittedly, on the surface, there may not be anything so terrible about the sound of this plan of action, and perhaps there isn't anything heinous about protecting the interests of corporate citizens per se, but I notice the language used to frame this predicament. Read the power invested in the entrenched economic values, in the force and might that these values have in lobbying for the removal of these people from the geography of the street. But why, do you think, is there a continual influx of panhandlers? What else might that be connected to, tangled in, fused with? What do they mean by unsightly? Unsightly to whom? What is accomplished by giving money to charities instead of directly to the end user? At least one interpretation could be that it aids in removing street people from the street scene and resettles them in social service institutions. Laura scoffs at the futility of the services available to her and suggests that "[putting] two million dollars from all the VLTs [video lottery machines] into like, the homeless shelters really doesn't do any good at all. Almost all the money that goes into the homeless shelters is being pocketed by the people that work there" (Laura, 10/05/98). Clearly social service agencies are more than simply repositories for the homeless and use their monies in more ways than just paying their staff. Certainly the staff who work in the services which aid street kids are well-intentioned people and do good work, but still there is something amiss in the land and institutions of the street. When I asked Gwen Danzig about the advice he would give to counselling services, he said, "Not sitting there and going, 'Ding, your time is up. Next'" (Gwen Danzig, 08/25/98). Now, however outlandish the interpretation offered is—that services on the street are aimed at removing homeless people from the landscape—it is nevertheless echoed in the accounts of how street kids understand the collusion among services, businesses, and public disdain. Discrete separations between how the kids size up those who don't want them sleeping in parks while they are jogging, and those who give care because they are paid for it, are not easily made by the kids. What I gleaned about what they were saying is that workers who must be paid to care (as opposed to care for free), and those whose money and privilege afford them the unthwarted opportunity to jog in parks in the morning, represent for the kids, two points on a continuum of mainstream economic values of materialism and instrumentalism. There is something to what Laura and Gwen Danzig have named, and something just doesn't seem to jive. It seems to me that they are talking about the everyday business 'of the shelters as an example of that which unintentionally perpetuates commodified relationships, relationships that I understand as further alienating street kids from the mainstream.

In another city, panhandling was cryptically described as "a significant social and safety concern," and a bylaw was passed "to ameliorate the negative impact of panhandling" (Bylaw 3M99, 1999) (see also Bylaws 6478, 6555/95, 7885 for similar ordinances regulating and restricting access and utilization of public space). But I wondered about what negative impact they were talking about? There was dissonance in my head as I tried to incorporate that which the kids told me with regard to their experiences of panhandling, and to also take up this other impression of what panhandling is based on the cities' perspectives. What kind of negative impact could panhandling possibly have on the street that is worse than the citizens of the place knowing that there are people who are having to panhandle?

The legal documents that authorize constraining, restricting, oppressing, and removing panhandlers (and squeegee-ers) from the streetscape are an impressive set of cultural artifacts to examine for language and intent, for what they say and for what they mean to say, for what is implied in the in-betweens of how they position, classify, and remand disenfranchised people to the periphery. In reading about the various rationales and discussions regarding panhandling, and loitering, and generally being a nuisance, I was dismayed to read how enmeshed governmental values were with those of private business enterprises as is exemplified in the case of the BIA of Vancouver. It always seemed to me that the interests of these two entities might, dare I say should, be different. As an example of how municipal governments want to ensure that the business of the city proceeds without interruption, the bylaws specify that panhandling is not to occur near banks, ATMs, near liquor stores, bus stops, or pedestrian walkways (see bylaws mentioned here). Ostensibly this is to protect the public from uncomfortable or potentially dangerous interactions with panhandlers. I think that we all can agree that protection of the public is not a bad value to have. But what troubles me, what I cannot figure out, what doesn't seem clear to me is how panhandling has come to be vilified in the way that it has. The explanation offered to me by the kids is that money, power, and position are what really underlie all that happens in, on, and around the landscape of the street and beyond.

Gibson (1998) sent this letter in response to yet another major city threatening to enact panhandling and squeegeeing bylaws:

> I understand that you are proposing an anti-panhandlers by-law. I am appalled by the heartless lack of understanding and compassion represented by your proposal.
>
> Panhandlers are not pretty. Panhandlers are not a joyous addition to street life. But regrettably, in Mike Harris's Toronto, they are an ever increasing fact of urban life.
>
> Undoubtedly, the police have adequate authority to deal with any aggressive or threatening people. They do not need more tools in their already bulging legal kit.
>
> As for prohibiting certain locations, I have always felt that panhandling outside liquor stores and banks was symbolically appropriate—even brilliant. Where better than outside a place specializing in luxuries like wine & spirits; or outside a place that dispenses cash to people who have cash?
>
> Please devote your energies to combatting the conditions that force people into begging in order to survive, not to intimidating, harassing, and otherwise maltreating some of the most vulnerable people in our society. (Gibson, 1998)

The bylaws delimiting kids' movement and freedom on the street focus on the very activities that kids use to subsist. I wonder how these bylaws help kids who are hungry. Like Jar said, "The agencies do need money to help us, but when all of the agencies are closed after nine o'clock and you're sitting there and you're like so hungry or something, you know, of course, you're going to panhandle" (Jar, 08/14/98). I wondered how mainstream agencies and municipal governments could honestly claim that they have real concern for the issues and obstacles that confront marginalized kids when everything about these laws suggests that, in fact, the opposite is the case. I wonder about how kids feel about being removed, herded, vilified, criminalized. Mike responds to the current move afoot to extricate him from the street:

> A lot of what I do is not…what I do that would be considered crime, is not what I would consider crime. I don't consider breaking into an abandoned house so I can go to sleep out of the snow or out of the rain a crime. I don't consider, you know, panhandling on the street for change so I can get something to eat a crime. And I don't consider walking out into the street with my squeegee and asking people if they want their windows cleaned a crime. (Mike, 10/08/98)

Framed as a criminal and, according to the law, a de facto offender, Mike rejects the burdensome imposition of the state in restricting his activities on the street and his adjudication as a thug. "I find a lot of street kids really don't like society. At least [not] the way society is fixed up and the structure of it," Gwen Danzig tells me. I ask him why. "It's bullshit, it makes me sick." I pry a bit more, "What about it?" I ask. "The people in it," he says. I ask again, "What about them?" He answers:

> Government. The things the political powers do, their decisions. It's like, I know that we live in one of the best countries in the world, but still there are so many things that our government does that are wrong. Awhile back Canada sold China a bunch of CANDU reactors. Our government doesn't care because it's money. There is not much of a big price on human life anymore. The government is missing a lot and they hate to admit it. Everybody does. It's like, we live in Canada and we're so great and everything. I hate to break it to you; Canada has poverty. (Gwen Danzig, 08/25/98)

I'm undone by the connections that he makes, by his political savvy, and taken aback by his condemnation of money as the epitome of our government's values. Political and economic order—all rolled up in one neat bundle—how nice.

Colonizing the Street: Economics and Exclusion

As we have noted, "[p]ublic spaces differ depending on their social, cultural, economic and symbolic functions, and, perhaps most importantly, depending on the meanings, contested and negotiated though they are, that different publics bring to them" (Lees, 1998, 251). It seems that political agendas are mingled with economic values and vice versa. Economic talk gets mixed into the messages, impressions, and interpretations that kids have about their lives on the street. Grub talks about the economic circumstances that face him as a street kid compared with the mainstream folk who nonchalantly walk by him.

> You know, lots of people think we're runaways and it's our own fault that we're on the streets and they don't care. They have problems like car payments or whatever to deal with [he says sarcastically], actually having something on their conscience about someone starving out on the streets in this cold weather [he shrugs], they don't care. (Grub, 11/02/98)

"The rich get richer and the poor get poorer. And it is a true philosophy" (Neil, 08/14/98). Money and status continually figure into how the kids perceive the mainstream and how they feel they are excluded from the spaces of the street. "I'm not useful for regular society, you know; I'm not a viable consumer because I have no money, and I'm not somebody who could buy a lot of things, so that makes me useless because this society is driven by money," Mike explains (Mike, 10/29/98). And Zena adds that part of her subjugation on the street comes from the distinctions in class and mobility that is afforded by money. "…[T]hey think that they're better because they make money and they have a place to live, but their love only comes from their money, and their hate comes from their money. You see, I think money is worthless. I think money is worthless." (Zena, 08/24/98)

> I don't know, the government right now is corrupt, and anybody who doesn't at least think, to some degree, that it is, is because, you know, they're serving their own interests and their own interests are money. But I mean, I think, a government like direct democracy, you know, that is probably the closest thing to a government that would actually work, but that's not the way it works anymore because the average citizen doesn't have a say in what goes on in his [sic] world. (Mike, 10/08/98)

"Capitalist power and its relations with politics are able to reproduce a morality that implies that certain people are better and more valuable than others on the basis of their place in the economic system" (Schissel, 1997, 14). This is so abundantly apparent in how street kids construct and understand their experiences of and on the street. Connections between selves, society, economics, and politics are all combined in what Mike offers about consumerism and homelessness.

> And they [being the "suits"—businesspeople] assume that because we don't sleep in a bed at night in a nice warm house, that we must be the scum of the earth, we must be the evil people. And it's because they're being manipulated by the media. I don't know, it's because, it comes down to money, it really does because we aren't consumers and media, and business don't like people who aren't consumers. If you don't buy a lot of stuff, you're not useful. I don't know. So that creates a big, they create a huge gap between the people who do buy a lot of stuff and the people who don't buy a lot of stuff. The people who don't buy a lot of stuff are looked down upon. The people who don't have TVs and the people who don't eat up all the ads are looked down upon because they don't fit into society. (Mike, 10/08/98)

Nicole also feels that she is not fitting into what the economic mainstream might require or allow for. She says that she is economically discriminated against because of her age. She isn't going to work at the "worst jobs for the worst money for no reason at all other than the fact that you're not old enough to work any of the good ones" and for the fact that she's homeless (Nicole, 09/02/98). So economic circumstances and class distinctions inscribe how kids come to interpret their world, making meaning and judgments about who they are, who we are, and about the discrepancies between our values.

A number of kids commented on the banality of the workaday world. Casting "suits" into a category apart from themselves, street kids articulate how their values are incongruent with what they perceive the values of the workforce to be. Gwen Danzig says: "You look outside and you see all these people and they are all just faceless people. They all walk around and they all look the same. Go and do the same thing [he pauses and scans the cityscape, nodding his head], and they are going nowhere" (Gwen Danzig, 08/25/98). Nicole says, "They build buildings, see this building, ugly and pointless. They build buildings to work in so that they can go home and live in their building. It just doesn't make any sense to me" (Nicole, 09/02/98).

They detect falsity in the constructed geography of the street and are able to reflect on the centrality of commodified relationships between themselves and the mainstream as a result of their marginalized position.

> They [suits] care about money. They don't care much about anything else. They care about their money and they care about their jobs. They pay taxes and they pay charities because the government says they have to or whatever, right? They don't care; they just want more money. More money, nice cars, big houses. Like I have a pillow and a sleeping bag, and maybe a girlfriend every once in awhile. And I am happier then they will ever be. (Crowchild, 09/02/98)

It isn't just the suits who might think about how their relationships with street kids are commodified; it is also helpers, adults, educators, parents, researchers, citizens, governments. Throughout my conversations with kids, it seemed that relationships free of the constraints and parameters of economic power differentials were the relationships that street kids felt the best about—for example, Jayne's (Chapter Three) comments on the kinds of friends that you can make on the street, or Gwen Danzig saying that if counselors are paid, then their caring has been diminished because it's been bought. For me specifically, trying not to commodify my relationship with the kids was critical. As I have stated, I wanted to give kids an opportunity not to be in a commodified relationship with me. Although I had been warned that kids wouldn't participate without the promise of payment, my research relationship needed to be based on mutual respect, trust, and understanding. There was going to be no compromise in how I modeled care in the brief time that I spent knowing these kids. I needed to proceed with integrity and that was that.

But despite my best intentions, one day I met with a kid for an interview, and I bought us each a coffee before settling in for our discussion. My notes record, as much as my gut remembers, how a simple cup of coffee changed the nature of our relationship. "All of a sudden, I was the buyer and he was the bought," I wrote (Me, 08/28/98). I didn't much like that, but, on the other hand, how could I sit across from kids and talk with them for a couple of hours without offering them so much as a cup of coffee? Those cold autumn afternoons and evenings I felt like a pig for being warm, and fed, and clothed. I would sit across the table from street kids, who I might have surmised were hungry, and I wouldn't offer to buy them anything to eat—even though I had the money—because I wanted my work to be "pure." That admission frightens and offends me. How could research ever be more important than the hunger of a kid? I struggled and squirmed under the weight of economic burdens that were placed on me and impinged on my relationships with the kids. Buying coffee represented a lot more than just buying coffee. Many months later, after learning that one of the street kids with whom I had developed a relationship had his sketchbook stolen, I replaced it without guilt or reproach. He was so touched by my gesture that he insisted on giving me a big hug. When the others saw that, they all joined in. We weren't commodified; we were just in a mutually respecting relationship.

It is evident that kids on the street grapple with economic issues beyond their own needs for sustenance. Since they have few ways to earn money other than the increasingly controlled and criminalized activities of panhandling and squeegeeing, one might imagine that a resentment could arise aimed at people who are upwardly mobile, or at least more economically advantaged than they are. That said, it seems that street kids referred to money and status more frequently in order to frame their experiences on the street as oppressed and marginalized persons. Connecting politics, economics, and social status to rights, privilege, justice, power, access, and entitlement, street kids took up the complexities of their lives by including the economic order to account for how it positions and impositions them in the streetscape.

Secrets of the Street: Police Brutality and The Moral Authority

There is a lot of nice cops, I have to admit that.
But at the same time
there is a lot of asshole cops,
especially in this city.
Seems like a lot of them, as soon as they get the badge on,
it's like I have the badge and you don't.
They go on this big power trip
because they got more authority. They abuse it.
(Gwen Danzig, 08/25/98)

And like the cops down here are real dicks.
There's like two good ones and the rest are just ignorant fucks,
like [they tell us] "you're street fucking rats," you know, they don't care.
(Jayne, 11/10/98)

Oh yea [I'm frightened]. More than anything,
the cops are the worst though.
They're the only ones that will actually beat us.
Like I'm usually scared to sleep somewhere.
Like if we find a good place to sleep,
the only thing that scares me is if the cops find us
because if they find you sleeping, they kick you.
They kick you in the head a good four or five times to wake you up.
And then if you ask them not to,
they'll like pick you up and strangle you
or fucking bend your arm back.
They're mean.
The cops here are so mean.
(Nicole, 09/02/98)

For a long time I didn't want to talk about it [police brutality].
Then I started to see the ages start younger and younger.
Like twelve, thirteen, fourteen. And like, I don't know.
I won't go to the paper or nothing but if someone asks me,
ya, I will tell them exactly what is going on.
Lot of cops are racists.
Like, if you are black, they will come up to you
and be harsher on you because you are black.
Because of your background. Or if you are Pakistani or whatever, right?
The same thing with the street kids, to them we are white trash.
Not worth anything. It bothered me at first,
but now it just doesn't bother me.
I won't trust anybody unless they are like, if they are a street kid.
I won't trust anybody but a street kid now.
Because they are the only people that
have treated me with the respect that I want.
You know? Everyone else just looks down at you because you are dirty.
You don't have showers, you sleep in alleys.
(Crowchild, 09/02/98)

You never know what will happen.
Someone could rob you or try and kill you in your sleep,
or you always get woken up by security guards
or cops kicking you out of places where you're sleeping.
Or it's cold and you got that thermal alarm clock
that wakes you up around 4:00 in the morning.
(Grub, 11/02/98)

You really don't want to run into troubles
because you get beat down harsh.
You can't walk and you are screwed
because all you're going to be able to do is lie there and bleed.
And I have seen a lot of homeless people
get beat harsh and they will be fucking sitting there,
asking for help. People will be just like, uh uh.
They are more worried about getting their suits dirty and stuff.
(Gwen Danzig, 08/25/98)

A bunch of powerful fucking assholes.
Yeah, the ones that are supposed to protect society
are the worst ones for us because
I guess we're not
a good enough part of society
for them.
(Nicole, 09/02/98)

Because most, I am not going to mention the names in this town
but there are certain cops in this town
that are really popular because they bust a lot of drugs
or they bust a lot of crime.
But while they are doing that,
they are beating the shit out of innocent people.
Just because they are lower class or they don't look right.
(Crowchild, 09/02/98)

The cops.
They think we're all just runaways and junkies,
and we're all out for no good.
We steal things and we have no respect
and blah, blah, blah.
Break into places and we do things just to make them mad,
but there's crack heads, and there's rapists, and wife beaters,
and all sorts of other worse things
that they could be spending their time on than wasting it on us,
like telling us to move from a place
we're sitting down and not doing anything anyway.
We were actually trying to earn our money
by squeegeeing, and then they give us fines.
(Grub, 11/02/98)

Street kids are often awakened by the brutal belts of police's hard
boots upon their sleeping bodies. This is known as "boot fucking." When
I heard about this I was shocked. After all, I had worked with street kids for
a number of years and had never known about this before. I couldn't

believe my ears, to be frank. This was not something I had read about in any depth in street kid literature,[13] and certainly physical police brutality, specifically, was not an issue being examined to any extent that I was aware of. Nothing could prepare me for the comments that kids made about being violated by public servants. "Modern policing is both pervasive and authoritative" (Herbert, 1998, 225), and that was made abundantly clear by the confessions kids made about it right from the outset.

"Police officers represent the most visible face of state authority, and work to achieve a seeming ubiquity across the space of the city" (Herbert, 1998, 225). But has their appropriation of space gone beyond our acceptable civil limit? These manifestations of street life were amazingly poignant for me in terms of seeing and understanding the experiences of kids in all their complications.

> Like stuff like police brutality. Like I mean, about two weeks ago my friend was arrested for trespassing in a public parking lot. He was in a parking lot [Mike says with emphasis, as if to reinforce the stupidity and excessive use of control of arresting a kid for being in a parking lot]. The cops arrested him for trespassing. They drove him out into the middle of nowhere and they threatened to stab him and his dog. And they're like, "Yeah, you guys are dirty street rats, what are you going to do, nothing, we can only put a choke hold on one of you at a time," and they were saying all this stuff and, I mean, I wish I had this with me [referring to my tape recorder] in my pocket at the time because that's, the police are here to protect us right, and the minute they stop doing their job they don't have a right to be there, and the police don't protect us. They're supposed to protect everybody but they're never around when you need them. I mean, the police serve their own interest just like everybody else. And it's just like, the government is there to serve the people, and once it stops serving the people and starts serving itself, it has no right to rule. (Mike, 10/08/98)

Street kids perceived the geopolitics of police brutality to be both unfair as well as state-sanctioned punitive oppression. The "...self-construction [of the police] as a morally driven defender of the good, the protector of order and peace in the streets" (Herbert, 1998, 229) is not what is understood by the kids about how police inhabit their place and position in the street. They deal with an altogether different kind of police force in

---

[13] See, for example: Baron, 1989; Bradley, 1997; Carlen, 1996; Plympton, 1997; Hagan & McCarthy, 1997.

the public spaces of the street. Wanting to "establish sovereignty over places of resistance" (Herbert, 1998, 230), police mete our harsh punishment to kids for occupying spaces that are considered out of bounds. Carlen (1996) names this as "political asymmetry," suggesting that "young people do not believe that police protection is extended to them in the same way that it is to older adults (especially older adults who are householders), and they also feel excluded from debates about the forms, functions, and possibilities of democratic policing" (2). She contends that even though the state is not meeting its responsibilities in terms of protecting and nurturing the young, homeless kids are nevertheless penalized for not fulfilling their citizenship obligations (read, being at home, invisible, and off the street) (Carlen, 1996). In some ways, police seem to treat street kids as if they are trespassing by being in the public terrain of the street. Like the criticism of the commodified agencies and the commentary that social service workers are nevertheless well-intentioned, so, too, can we extend that assumption to the police—probably. But the kids spoke clearly about a police force that they perceive as hostile and unjust. Kids figure out through their experiences on the street that these people are not to be trusted and that the police ultimately govern in the interests of the state, on behalf of the businesses, and, ultimately act, as arbiters of public space.

Moral Panics and Folk Devils: Demonizing Youth on the Street

What I have attempted to show throughout this chapter is how street kids are connected to, and disenfranchised from, the systems which affect their lives on the street. From all vantage points—political, personal, municipal, governmental, philosophical, spatial, geographical, and economic—kids are vilified, brutalized, and criminalized out of the public spaces of the streetscape. Homeless youth are increasingly occupying contested and negative spaces in the popular imagination (see, for example, Carlen, 1996; Giroux, 2000; Ruddick, 1996, 1998; Schissel, 1997). In addition to the privatization of public space which constricts kids' movements and freedoms and the capitalist values which permeate the actions and relationships to which street kids feel connected, the street has become a site for kids' political struggles and for struggles of self and identity both overt and covert. Although there is no evidence in the literature to suggest that kids come to the street for political reasons per se, I wondered if it may be that they stay on the street because in so doing they find their political voices, either through resistance to political, economic, or social doctrine, or simply by occupying the contested spaces of the street. Because I had heard so much about how kids sized up mainstream society, and because so much of who they are seemed to be indivisible from their interconnected relationships with larger order systems, I wondered whether being on the street for some time, existing and hovering in the contested spaces of the street, and coming to understand more about the economic, political, and social order of Western society enabled street kids to read the complicated textures and intricacies of dominant ideologies in a way that we don't or can't. Pipher (1994) suggests that because adolescents are so vilified in Western culture, they often identify with underdog causes in order to express their repressed political ideals (e.g., animal rights, environmental issues). Perhaps this may especially be so for street kids, if, by their own physical presence on the street, they see themselves as subversive agents resisting, contesting, and interrupting dominant-culture values. Gwen Danzig stated "that [not liking mainstream's values] is why a lot of street kids stay on the street." He said:

> Like, a lot of us would like phones and everything but at the same time we don't want to be a part of society. I don't know, it's funny. My one friend put it in weird terms; all the punks should get together and burn the buildings to the grounds. Then we will go to the hippies and rebuild. (Gwen Danzig, 08/25/98)

Kids appeared deeply connected to, and profoundly invested in taking up, the social, political, and economic conditions that affect them in their lives as street kids. Power and money, politics, oppression and space, brutality, freedom, justice, and hope are the facets of a politically saturated street life to which street kids spoke a great deal in their conversations with me. Illuminating the tremendous inequities and oppressions with which they contend, street kids' stories seemed to condemn a mainstream apathy, intolerance, and culpability which, in effect, has no positive effect in altering the conditions of their homeless lives. Charging that dominant ideologies reify and perpetuate the status quo, street kids commented on the moral bankruptcy of mainstream culture. Exposing the oppressive ideologies and the punitive systems that operate in marginalizing and alienating kids on the street, the investigation into the experiences of street kids broadened, and, ultimately, so did the stakes.

Chapter Five

The Jagged City Frame

I went downtown but it was really quiet. I saw Jayne. We talked about whether or not she wanted to join me sometime for an interview. She seemed reluctant. She said that she is a very private person. I saw Mike too. He had some writing with him. He had told me before that he didn't want me to read it in front of him. I took his book into the McDonald's and sat down.

Five pages of writing. I read each page with care, care like holding a delicate snowflake—fragile, careful careful.
It was like…I felt voracious.
Beautiful, tragic, painful, exquisite.
I was teary, a lump in my throat the size of a goiter.
I sat in the McDonald's awhile to take it in. To appreciate what he had shared with me, what private domain he had let me enter.
I sat quietly and sadly, and felt the full weight of a society gone awry, of misplaced persons and displaced dreams.
I cried a little and thought how bourgeois to be crying about this
        kid's plight.
But I knew that I was crying for me too!
I sat and thought and reflected for a long while…
Cherishing a kind of closeness with him. There was something different about him giving me his book, yes, something different than our conversations together. (Me, 11/05/98)

I went outside and felt speechless. Eagerly, he asked, "So what did you think?" I replied, "I don't know what to say, you write beautifully." He asked again, "Do you want to use any of them?" His face expressing the potentiality of a rejection response—wondering "Is this any good?" read, "Am I any good?" I answered, "Yes, yes I would like all of them, if I can?" His face illuminated. There was a kind of bashfulness of a sort that indicated that he was surprised by my positive reaction, as if he hadn't heard anything positive about himself in a long time, as if no one had remembered to say anything nice to him for the length of eternity.

I said, "This writing is outstanding. I'm a little teary, it made me cry." He was shocked. "It did?" he asked, almost blushing. I said "yes" and touched him on his head. "If I could make the world a better place for you, I would," I said softly, stupidly, tritely.

And with that we understood each other differently than we had before. Amazed by his expression, awed by his ability to write, I walked a little way to photocopy the pages of his poetry and breathed deeply in.

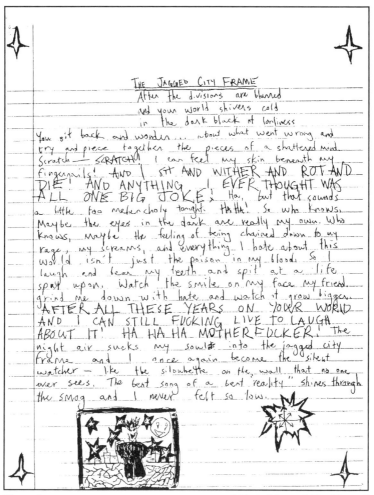

Figure 1   *Mike's "Jagged City Frame"*

There isn't much to say when the words of the silenced are suddenly screaming raucously in your head, when the images and languages of others strike you and initiate you and capture you. With prose, the wine of words, Mike drinks his experience of the street and sets it down, lays it out, bares his soul. "The Jagged City Frame" frames it beyond what we can articulate about the experiences of the street for kids. His words and images and thoughts are irreducible, exact, raw.

There is so much to think about, or say, or contemplate about all that Mike has spoken in this piece. I want to speak to it and stamp my feet, and scream, and cry, and bring to bear all that is invested in his writing. But I also want to be silent and let the echoes of his work boomerang endlessly inside me. I want his words to be cast off like sails into the breeze floating gently into our consciousnesses or ravage our preconceptions like the deadly winds of tornados ripping us from our complacent circumstances. I want his words to unlock our suffocated languages, to break open our smallness, our egos, our hearts. I want him to reach us, teach us, remind us, heal us. I want him to be present so that the connections that he draws are considered in the paths that we follow, that we explore and investigate. Most of all, I want his words to be his.

The Harvest of Commodities and Filling Up Our Talk

This chapter is offered for three reasons. First, I wanted to share Mike's writing with you. I wanted him to have a chance to be recognized on his own. Second, I wanted to offer you an alternative experience in understanding street kids' lived experiences by this poetic offering. I think that his writing is spectacular, sacred, special, crucial, intense, critical. And, third, I needed to offer Mike's writing in a way that would feel respectful of its totality, but I had a lot of difficulty putting it in any other space other than its own. Like sites of struggle for street kids, their words need to occupy alternative spaces, subversive and different, and precious locales that are open to hearing them. I chose to provide one, to honor that which is unique and special about this writing, about this kid, about this soul. Yet even my best attempts to clear a small space for Mike seem onerous and difficult and just a bit out of sync. But this has been the case all along.

It seems that every time I weave together the words and experiences of street kids for academic consumption, it feels like I dismantle a little bit of what they have said. Each time I tie something together or make connections, I also depreciate the enormous power and impact of the words street kids have spoken. Although I am not claiming that my grappling with this issue is a problematic of representation, that somehow by weaving the words of street kids with my own I am defiling what is pure about what they have said (hermeneutic work does not make that claim), I still wince in the actions of writing, and interpreting, and reflecting. Making their words more than what they are seems like sacrilege. Their words speak volumes by themselves perhaps even more eloquently than what I can say around them.

Voices from the margins have hardly been heard, have hardly entered the hectic discourses that operate in and on the topic of the street, and in the very instant that they do, we somehow rob their words by explaining them away, by connecting them to bigger things, by evaluating and analyzing them for their productive and generative qualities. On the one hand, the synergy between multiple perspectives between all conversants affords questions and curiosities to emerge unfettered. That polyphonic conversation is what interpretive research is all about. It is precisely the renovation of the topic through dialogic discussions that lead us, and take us, and beckon us. On the other hand, there is something about an academic hegemony that compels us to appropriate people's languages, words, constructions, ideas, beliefs, and harvest them for some kind of benefit.

Despite the altruistic goal of visioning something new about a topic, of reaching some different understanding about ourselves and the world in which we live by opening new dialogues for conversation, research can be brutal and perhaps unintentionally presumptuous. Street kids are being silenced in so many more ways than I can possibly lay out here, and it is precisely here that I query whether or not I have become a silencing agent as well? Sixel (1988) tells his story this way: "...my fieldwork had allowed me to harvest a few commodities (in essays and papers) from my case-studies with which I could enter the marketplace of academic exchange in the hope of making a few modest gains" (Sixel, 1988, 1). Interesting to name the university as an academic marketplace. Hmm.

> We always spoke about repression, exploitation, and the Proletarian Revolution without ever reaching more than a few of those who have rightfully been called our "Pet Proletarians." Mostly, we spoke to ourselves about our own problems by using the problems of others to fill up the emptiness of our talk. We seldom raised the question of what was wrong with us and why we could not make sense to others. (Sixel, 1988, 2)

And there it is, stated as the academic problem and ethical dilemma that it is and has become for me. Conceiving of street kids as my "Pet Proletariat" makes me feel ill. I hope that isn't me and know that my hopes are inevitably tied up in the naive conception of making the world a more aware and tolerant, loving and peaceful place. Nevertheless, I engage the uncomfortable position that I live as a researcher and cloak myself in the discomfort of that positioned identity.

So what shall I do? Shall I leave Mike's "Jagged City Frame" for your contemplation without saying anything more? Or will I speak to it as it transports me in a million directions beyond itself? These are the choices with which I am left.

"The Jagged City Frame" Interpreted

Mike's eloquence moves me. I'm in awe and at a loss. I don't want to undo all that he has cast in his poetry and to explain it so that its power is reduced, but I also need to attend to what possibilities this encounter might offer. And so this work is presented here in the spirit of renovation, of coming back again to the familiar, to hear again, differently, what life on the street for kids is like. "Interpretive inquiry thus begins with being 'struck' by something, being 'taken' with it" (Jardine, 1992, 55), and I was likewise captured by his piece, by his articulation, by his deliverance, because I experienced it to be the articulation of the whole that encapsulated the various parts of this unfolding story.

Reading his poetry, there is a sense of oppressiveness that is unmistakable and that connects me to all the pieces and parts of what I laid out in the previous two chapters about life on the street for kids. For me,

"The Jagged City Frame" is the reflection of a world in which the other is reviled, outcast, erased. The world is cold, and he's alone with his thoughts and rage, alone in a world that separates him, that he also understands as separated. He tells us that he is dying, and I wonder if he is dying like the fragile souls who are being ignored on the street. Is he dying from loneliness? Is he dying from living under the weight of "other," from being erased and unwanted? The possible ways he might be becoming undone are countless, and endless, and are inextricably set in the confusion about how the totality of this scene has come to be.

In our reading of his poetry, the divisions between "us" and "them" become visceral. Oppression is named, and everything in the night sky seems remarkably clear. Like the frame on the page, Mike offers a snapshot in which vision is restored and connections can be made, connections that kids shared with me throughout our conversations together.

Casting himself in the lonely, dark night, Mike lays the boundaries for his life as a street kid and situates himself firmly on one side. He is accompanied by his rage, rage that is unnamed and untamed. Perhaps there is too much to say. He knows what it is that enrages him, but he doesn't say it. He leaves us wondering what it could be. He can feel it, live it, speak it, know that it is growing, even by not naming it. I query the joke to which Mike refers set in and against the pressure building in the jagged city frame, and wonder if he is speaking to his lost ideals, if he is articulating the distances between himself and other, if the "big joke" refers to parts of himself that he feels are not valued or are being lost. Are those the ransoms kids pay for existing in the margins? What will we do if that is indeed the case? Eyes in the dark are watching him. He can't make out whose they are and asks if they are his own. Like the ambiguity that exists in the confused spaces of the street, where contested identities are made and re-made, street kids struggle to know what to make of themselves and others, what to make of things that are present to them in their circumstances on the street. It's not in his head, this separation that he feels; he knows what he is feeling is "real." He conveys his sentiments by suggesting, "it's not my imagination; I haven't constructed my homeless oppression all by myself or in my head." Living in the difficult and uncomfortable spaces of marginalization, Mike understands himself as the "watched" and warns of his growing hatred. What will that mean for him? For us? Is the jagged city omnipotent? Can it really see him, know him, account for him, love him? Can it take responsibility for his hate? Will it even share? He hovers, like the stories of kids interpreting what street life is like, in the tensions between his own power and his own powerlessness.

Strong words and images also reject oppression and instead spit back "at a life spat upon." He's laughing at us, he knows what we're made of, what we've made the world; he condemns us with his tone. His hatred is growing; it will be a force to be reckoned with. But no amount of rage or hate seems to be able to save him from retreating into "The Jagged City Frame" as a silenced soul. Though his silhouette has not lost the power to be a "silent watcher," "The Jagged City Frame's" force is too much for him to bear and ultimately "sucks his soul," rendering him invisible. Those silenced voices are paying careful attention; they are aware of the encounters in the city; they can tell us and can talk to us about life on the street because they see it from a different vantage point. They are watching us but are unable to stop us from hurting them because they have been silenced. The "bent reality" of this life we cannot see without a guide. We are uninvited because we've been named and numbed in the alienated and alienating place.

We cannot escape how this writing implicates us as co-creators of "The Jagged City Frame." Perhaps this poem is precisely the invitation that we need to unhinge what might be difficult for us to see, or hear, or cope with. For me, these aren't just the words of a reluctant hero, romanticized and severed from the daily toils of the street. This poem is about the very down-to-earth circumstances that problematize Mike's life as a street kid. It is in this way that its power is revealed to me and sets it apart for me. Stark images and words resound in what I have come to understand as the significations of life on the street for kids. This eloquence is the vehicle through which we are transported to imagine how these circumstances, along with the connected explorations of Chapters Three and Four, might be possible.

Interpreting Interpretation

"The interpreter always approaches the object of interpretation with a

question built into her [sic] *very approach" (Gallagher, 1992, 155), and so, I offer this interpretation in response to how Mike's powerful words are connected to what I've understood street kids have been telling me about their lives. I offer it as an instance of importance, as an embodied example of the totality of their lives, calling me back to and beyond the intricacies of life on the street for kids. When I read it, it spoke to me about the uncomfortable spaces of the street that I've been grappling with throughout this book. My first response to it was to write prose about how it moved me (see beginning of this chapter), because the experience of reading it was so intense that poetry seemed like the appropriate form and forum to respond to what I had just received. Intellectualizing it and connecting it up to the greater issues that reverberated within it was not my first concern. I recognized Mike's prose as an expression of the stories and tales, of the learning and exploring I had embarked on all those months ago. It reverberated because in it I found what was familiar and also what was new. Now, however, in this space of academic scholarship, I am called upon to give it voice, to read into the text that has come before it, and invite it into the world of possibilities to which it has yet to summon us.*

There is a tension that lives in the act of interpretation, that I named earlier, in which I continue to feel caught. On the one hand, re-enlivening this text beyond its severed borders, in other words not allowing Mike's words to be his and only his, is the way that it can be generative, fruitful, lead us to greater questions and further understandings as I've tried to offer. Making it live again is how it will teach us and open us to thoughts well beyond its individual borders. On the other hand, offering an interpretation as I have done here runs the risk of trivializing his work, making it flat, reducing it, or making it trite. There seems to be a risk in interpreting it, a risk that lives in the tension between good interpretation and sentimentalization. I am not fearful of not being able to reproduce what the author intended—that is not a hermeneutic tenet—but rather I'm fearful that my interpretations might be themselves limited, and trite, and somehow superfluous, and might, therefore, limit the connections which could be generated by the reader who has also read the previous two chapters. As Gadamer concedes (1997), "[c]onceptual explication is never able to exhaust the content of a poetic image" (39). Smith (1994) says "[G]ood interpretation shows the connection between experience and expression" (107), but I am humbled to bring expression to what is experienced through Mike's prose. "The Jagged City Frame" was offered to me as a whole, as an expression of its own, and so it feels somehow different to connect it back and forth into the multitude of ways that it speaks about the lived experiences of street kids as opposed to how I've been able to do that with the transcripts that were generated in my conversations with kids on the street.

A second tension that arises by taking up this text resides in the opposing spaces of academic consumerism on one side (Sixel, 1988), and academic good intention on the other, as I have also mentioned. It is a kind of double bind because in addition to the connections that we can draw and the possibilities the text can open for us, we also have to reckon with the differential power relations that are invested in the identities of street kid and scholar, respectively. In my invested position, I can open up the space for Mike's words to be read into, and between, what has come before. Not only can I, but I did, and I am. But there is a discomfort in doing that, at every instance, because one interpretation of so doing is that it positions me as the emancipator of his words. In Chapters Three and Four, the interpretive act felt comfortable, natural, significant. Maybe I was both emancipator and explorer there too. In this instance, I'm a little less at ease with the task of interpretation. Maybe I'm trying to balance my scholarly commitment to understand something new about the lived experiences of street kids with my belief that street kids can speak eloquently for themselves. Maybe I need to learn more about how to temper when I want to retreat from the role of emancipator, colonizer of words and ideas from the street, and when it feels right, worthy, ethical, and important to acknowledge my powered spot and push open the spaces for marginalized voices to be heard. For now, I can only offer "The Jagged City Frame," my attempted connections and interpretations of it, and all the surrounding questions that I have about power, voice, research, and academics.

Chapter Six

Prophetic Visionings

> We and the prophet have no language in common. To us the moral state of society, for all its stains and spots, seems fair and trim; to the prophet it is dreadful. So many deeds of charity are done, so much decency radiates day and night; yet to the prophet satiety of the conscience is prudery and flight from responsibility. Our standards are modest; our sense of injustice tolerable, timid; our moral indignation impermanent; yet human violence is interminable, unbearable, permanent. To us life is often serene, in the prophet's eye the world reels in confusion. The prophet makes no concession to man's *[sic]* capacity. Exhibiting little understanding for human weakness, he *[sic]* seems unable to extenuate the culpability of man *[sic]*. (Heschel, 1962, 9)

The prophets in our midst are those whose visions permit them to see things otherwise. It is for prophets that we wait, hoping to find a better way, a clearer path, a new horizon on which to set our sights. They are the voices that call us to higher ideals and that show us how narrow our vista has been. Prophets connect things that we cannot imagine, that are too difficult, or scary, or painful to synthesize into our daily lives but that nevertheless need to be reconciled. They set a new course for our imagination and aim to awaken our moral sensibilities to the social injustices of the time.

But prophets are often misunderstood, reviled, cast out. Their visionings are often set against the dominant ideologies or the predominant methods of the time. Heschel (1962) suggests that

> [t]he prophet is human, yet he *[sic]* employs notes that are one octave too high for our ears. He *[sic]* experiences moments that defy our understanding. He *[sic]* is neither "a singing saint," nor "a moralizing poet," but an assaulter of the mind. Often his *[sic]* words begin to burn where conscience ends. (10)

I wonder if prophets speak in octaves too high, or whether we have stopped straining our ears to hear their voices. Who are the prophets of our time? To whom would we listen, whom would we, or do we, authorize to set our collective agenda? How much a part of that agenda have we participated in setting? Who is calling us to account for and think about the practices of our lives?

In light of what Heschel (1962) says about who prophets are and what they can see, perhaps we might re-vision how we might take up that which street kids have pointed us to, summoned us to see, connected for us in terms of their lives and ours. Perhaps, like prophets, street kids name pieces and parts of our living together that are uncomfortable, and painful, and frightening to face, both for them and for us. We don't need to romanticize them excessively or valorize them as having more than mortal vision, but maybe we could listen to them in different ways than we have; maybe we might acknowledge their unique horizon of sight.

The visions that street kids shared with me about their lives on the street have been woven into the text that you have read. In their tellings and mine, I have tried to show how their world is framed in the contested spaces of the street, how their experiences are tangled in the webs of economic, social, and political contexts, how panhandling is the embodied experience of their lives on the street, and how all of this converges in the tentatively constituted identities of street kids and ourselves that somehow inform the meanings of all of this, for all of us. I believe that they've called on us to account for the ways in which we live our lives by speaking about theirs, especially as they take notice of the systems that we abide. I have tried to connect kids' narratives to the predominant values imbedded in the larger systems to see how the values undergird and overwrite those narratives, to see what is informed, and what is informing the experiences of life on the street for kids.

Between the Sacred and the Profane

The complexities that kids face on the street are staggering as we have seen. The kids vacillate in the in-betweens of life, swirling in the tensions that abound in their world as was exemplified in exploring how their experiences on the street are simultaneously constructed as good, bad, and in between. They take up difficult issues—such as politics, economics, philosophy, and sociology—because they have no comforts to numb them away from the questions of life and living that confront them in their daily lives as street kids. They struggle to understand the cruelty of their world by vilifying the systems which have rejected them. By speaking to the values, ethics, and morals imbedded in those systems, they try to make sense of their lives in opposition, as the "other." In all of that, in the midst of the confusion, in the midst of both loving and hating their street experiences, they also managed to speak about the kinds of values that they respect and commit to, even if only tentatively, even if they can't always live up to those ideals. They are human too, and flawed like the rest of us. Between the good and the bad of the street, between being cast out and finding an alternative community, between the sacred and the profane of what they understand and experience, kids shared their thoughts with me about how it ought to be, how they'd like it to be, how they would restore our alienated social order to values that bespeak respect, kindness, and community.

> We all lean on each other, you know, it's like a teepee and, you know, I really, really love it because it's probably the closest thing I've found to actual unity in this society because, you know, if we don't stick together, then we're nothing. (Mike, 10/08/98)

Street life is comprised of a lot of hardship as we've noted in exploring street kids' experiences of being panhandlers, in the increasingly limited spaces and places that are available to them in the "public" domain, and in the economic and political systems which they interpret as being both oppressive and repressive. Their identities as homeless kids seem to be discursively constituted and confused as a result of the intersections between themselves and their interactions in the limbo spaces of the street, between their agency and their docility. But Mike tells us that despite those conditions, and maybe even because of them, street kids work collaboratively to enhance their lives on the street together, and that there is value in unity.

Social support systems and street families have been somewhat acknowledged in the literature in terms of the their importance in mitigating the hardship of life on the street (see, for example, Bradley, 1997; Brannigan & Caputo, 1993; Lundy, 1995; Plympton, 1997), but I am being called to hear something else in what Mike is telling me. I have turned here to listen for the ethical or moral messages imbedded in what he is telling me, to listen for the notes an "octave too high" in his narrative. I have no doubt that the instrumental tasks and connections between street kids forged in the spaces of the street are critical components in understanding street life for kids, but there is a risk of nullifying what they say by focusing too narrowly on tasks and specifics. This [un]raveling of street kids' experiences began in the specifics of panhandling and spiraled into the larger questions and issues of economics, politics, social structure, and morality, which connect the details with the larger pieces. As Jardine (1992) explicates, exploring the "fecundity of the individual case" "reveal[s] something to us about our lives together" (55). I was hearing something different in what Mike was telling me about his experience, something that doesn't only have to do with communing with people for how they can serve you, but rather how living in a community, under difficult circumstances, has served him as an experiential lesson in cooperation and collaboration. Ruddick (1996) speaks about the tactics of being on the street in terms of both the literal and symbolic meanings that kids ascribe to their experiences there. But she cautions that in trying to understand what goes on in the street by only examining the tactics of the kids, there is a risk of normalizing and romanticizing kids' actions by confining them to the identities of runaway or homeless. This narrow view excludes an appreciation of the meanings and connections that street kids make, as well as the identities that they develop in the spaces of the street. What if that was true of much of what kids say to us in our daily experiences with them? In other words, what if what Mike said was not only about the instrumental tasks of street socialization processes but rather was a clue to how he revisions the world and his place in it? I was attending to possibilities, and so it goes that the voices of street kids filled my tape recorder with tellings about how their circumstances on the street were difficult and how, as a result of those experiences, they had become different people with values anchored in different things. Zena says:

> [P]eople out here, they love because they love, because they are there, and

they care. They don't put themselves on pedestals. They know that everybody is just the same as them, you know. People might have more problems or not have any problems at all, but people on the streets are the same anyway. It doesn't matter how long you've been on the streets, what you do. If you're a hooker, you still get respected the same. (Zena, 08/24/98)

Gwen Danzig offers this about the values that, at the very best of times, he ascribes to in his life on, and beyond, the street.

It's like helping each other out when they need help. And basically thinking for yourself and making your own decisions. And knowing what is right from wrong. And what not to do. [The street is] [j]ust more about unity and peace and not all the bullshit of being harassed by the government and corporates and stuff. It's living more freely (Gwen Danzig, 08/27/98). [Being on the street] [y]ou appreciate life a lot more. You appreciate the experiences you can take in life whether they are good or bad. And just learn that there is more to life than just keeping yourself alive and going to work. (Gwen Danzig, 08/25/98)

And Mike again:

I like who I am, you know. But the way I see it is that, being like this, being myself, having my own mind and doing my own thing, it's a way to find the people who really matter, or the people who are willing to look past what I look like and to respect me and the fact that I have my own mind. I'd rather have one friend who will let me be who I want, than other friends who want me to be exactly like them because, I don't know, real friends are what…and being homeless is actually how you find out who your real friends are. (Mike, 10/08/98)

Neil says, "I mean, we need more love in the world. We need less division" (Neil, 11/12/98). How can I argue? I take him at his word.

There is no doubt about how idealistic the preceding comments are. There is no contestation that in the face of despair kids can envision alternative solutions to their plights, as we have heard throughout their explications of life on the street. But I am willing to be idealistic with them, to strain my ear to hear them, to listen all the time for possibilities in what they are telling me. Katz (1998) concludes that "[t]he environments of youth speak to them of the future…[i]t is important to take seriously what it means to them as they construct their identities and make place" (141). I tend to agree, believing that, from places beyond the borders of the mainstream, kids have a lot to teach us.

> The aim of interpretation, it could be said, is not just another interpretation
> but human freedom, which finds its light, identity, and dignity in those few
> brief moments when one's lived burdens can be shown to have their source
> in too limited a view of things. (Smith, 1994, 102)

This is what I'm listening for, this is what I'm hearing, and this is what I'm trying to do. Similarly, I think kids were interpreting their experiences on the street for possibilities. Where are the ruptures in the stereotypes of street life for kids that we, and they, can push through and break open? What do they know about freedom and dignity that we have yet to learn or have forgotten? And so, I am led to wonder how they manifest these ideals in their lives on the street in action, in praxis. In the particularities of the street, for example, I learned about the rules and ethics of panhandling, but how are their lofty ideals of freedom and peace translated in the conditions of the street?

From Ideology to Action

In addition to how street kids commented about their circumstances of the street, and how they idealize about how life could be, or ought to be, kids also shared with me the tensions around putting ideology into action.

> There is lots of us that would like to do stuff like, start organizations to help
> other people out and stuff. But nobody really wants to take the time to listen
> or care. You know they got their problems, "Sorry, we can't help." People
> don't care for each other anymore. Seriously, human rights may have gone
> up a little bit. Black rights have gone up plus various things happening in the
> last hundred years. But fucking people just don't care anymore. They stick
> to their own little cliques. If you are not settled then you are not one of them
> and just, sorry. (Gwen Danzig, 08/25/98)

Gwen Danzig seems to articulate his frustration in not being able to "start organizations to help other people." But his will seems to be there—seems present in striving to make the world a better place.

> It is getting too fast paced [talking about society]. Honestly, I believe that

humans discovered their technology way too quick. In the last hundred
years we have gained knowledge that you are not ready to use. Atomic
power, nuclear power. That stuff I think should have tooken us hundreds
of years more before we obtained it. We do not respect that nearly enough.
Look at Chernobyl. Thousands of acres gone to waste for thousands of
years. Like you can't even set foot there or you are going to die. We rape
the natural resources. We rape the earth so bad. (Gwen Danzig, 08/25/98)

Gwen Danzig laments the confused world of economics, politics, and the
environment, perhaps acknowledging his own impotence to solve, or be
helpful in, the greater transnational issues of environmental devastation.
But, what seems interesting to me is that he nevertheless accepts part of the
blame by naming himself in the "we" who "rape the natural resources." It
seems to me that kids philosophize about greater world issues because they
see them as deeply connected to their lives. Alluding to things that on the
surface seem to have little to do with the instrumental tasks of his daily life
on the street, Gwen Danzig makes a connection between how he lives as a
street kid and the environmental and human catastrophe of Chernobyl.
There is a kind of solidarity between the marginalized kids of the street and
the exploited environments or oppressed groups with which they identify.
Again, the risk of undervaluing this concern and this articulation cannot be
overstated. It isn't only that they identify with these causes because they are
oppressed; it is also because they see things differently and because they
want to set things "right." Massey (1998) notes that "the construction of
spatiality can be an important element in building a social identity" (128),
and this is realized in what Gwen Danzig is summarizing in the cultural
ecology and political economy of himself as a street kid, and Chernobyl as
part of his immediate concern.

Learning about street kids' prophetic visions didn't seem to be about
simply making their circumstances better on the street. These possibilities
were not centered in the narrow space of ameliorating their conditions only.
Street kids seemed invested in changing both their own circumstances and
the conditions of the world around them. In their limited positions of
power, with their beleaguered senses of agency, street kids often protest
and parade, calling on others to join them in the quest for a better life. For
example, in one city, street kids presented the mayor with a bucket of dead
fish and the "Illustrious award for Most Crimes Committed Against the

Community" (Macdonald, 1999). The Golden Squeegee Committee commented that in addition to not meeting the needs of street kids in a myriad of ways (e.g., lack of commitment to support services for kids, thereby limiting services for kids under eighteen years of age, police harassment of panhandlers and squeegee-ers, city council restricting youth gatherings—considering them loitering), the city council also refuses to "clean up the Belle Park pollution problem even after being fined." The committee stated that "...we are supposed to have a right to free speech. It is the responsibility of the local government to listen and take action in the best interests of all citizens, not just in the interests of business owners and governments because certain issues inconvenience them" (Macdonald, 1999).

Examples like these serve to underscore the issues of community and possibility that I am trying to raise. Street kids seem to be representing more than themselves. They are also representing the environment and those whose voices seem to get lost in the hectic fray of the urban landscape.

Other manifestations of kids trying to make their world, and, through action, our world, a better place include volunteering in certain organizations. Mike's commitments lie in serving food to hungry people for an activist not-for-profit peace group. He spoke about it this way:

> [I participated in] a Food Not Bombs Convention here, and it was like an activist convention. Every Saturday, they cook up a whole bunch of food that's donated to them, and then they go down to The Plaza and they serve it to anyone who's hungry. And I'm a part of it, like I help cook it and serve it, and stuff like that. (Mike, 10/08/98)

I found it to be a very telling story that some hungry kids find it important to volunteer for other hungry people. "I'm a part of it," he said. I took that to mean "this is part of my identity" or "I practice what I preach." What this said to me is that kids care an awful lot about looking after each other, and about looking after the planet as well. Certainly, as we have heard, they are critical of us and of the "system," but in the small spaces where they can contribute, they seem to try to make the world a better place by being agents of change in it. Mike says "anger is a good thing, anger is the first step in changing anything that you don't like"

(Mike, 10/08/98).

> I think if a lot more people knew why they were angry, then things would be
> a lot different because, you know, but either they just don't take the time to
> actually figure it out or they don't care. If you can pinpoint the things that
> piss you off then…if you can realize the higher powers out there, I guess, that
> are manipulating you and the people out there that are using you for your
> money and the media that wants you to, you know, the media controls a lot
> of people and it shapes almost entirely who they are…and pretty soon we're
> going to blow up the whole world and we're going to poison it so bad that
> we can't even live here anymore and we're going to have a fist full of dollars
> right after we take our last breath of poison air and it's not worth it. It's
> totally not worth it. (Mike, 10/28/98)

And so again the environment is mangled under the dominion of
economics. Is Mike invoking these as the symbols of our carelessness, of
our dimmed morals, hopes, and ethics? What is he is speaking to that is
represented in nature? I imagine that in some ways his experience on the
street is echoed in other silenced voices; that is, he is being
disenfranchised, forgotten, and disconnected from the rhythms of
mainstream life.

I'd like to believe that they have something to say in all of this, that
they are offering possibilities in terms of their own lives on the street but
also, and most importantly, for how we might reorient ourselves given what
they are saying. Crowchild says:

> People [should] start caring. Like the country Canada, the States, all over the
> world. The governments they just ignore them [kids]. Like the children that
> people bring [into the world] they just ignore them. They let them starve on
> the street. (Crowchild, 09/02/98)

Poverty, torture, rights of children, these are no ethereal concepts to kids
on the street. These issues are about them and beyond them. In our
conversations, street kids seemed serious about the ills of the world and
their concern for people worse off than even themselves. I believe that they
were trying, in earnest, to provide me with a new vision of what and who
they are, and how and why our society should be otherwise. Like the
prophets admonishing the clan, like the seer who tries to shape the future,
street kids are calling us.

I guess the one most appealing thing to me would be to open a bunch of people's eyes, "Hey, look. Look around you. There is a lot of bullshit out there and everything is not perfect. It's time to do something about it." (Gwen Danzig, 08/27/98)

Visions Forward and Back

It has been a long journey and the road extends in many directions far into the distances of possibilities. I am ready now to give pause, to reflect, to let these ideas and connections turn and change and take me beyond where I have been. This inquiry has been about the lives of street kids, but it has also not been about street kids at all. Rather, it's been about you and me, about who we are, about who street kids see us to be, and about who we all might otherwise like to be. It is about us, as we engage together—knowingly or unwittingly, consciously or inadvertently—in the creation and co-creation of the social, political, economic, and cultural landscapes that construct, are constructed by, and oppress kids. It's about the geographies that kids inhabit, emotionally, physically, spiritually, and politically. This work is about them as they reflect to us about us and acknowledges the unavoidable dichotomy of the "us" and "them" that we all live with. They feel it, they know it, they live it, and, sadly, so do we.

I want to comment on two elements of the "us" and "them" dichotomy. The first is related to the rigid separation between societal castes which street kids clearly articulated in their narratives, and which have served to discriminate between them and others (as I've tried to show throughout this book). The second is how that dichotomy positions me to be in an alliance with the mainstream, a position I am uncomfortable with. I have reflected, talked, and thought about street kids as a "something," but something is always set against something else. I've tried to avoid getting caught up in arguments condemned to binary opposites and the like, and have tried to stay out of the limited spaces of extremes. I have not found a place in this terrain where I can be comfortable—I am neither a street kid nor an eagerly participating agent of the mainstream status quo, and, despite my learning and coming to understand something new about street kids, I am not settled in the complexities of this terrain. Perhaps this uneasiness is somehow connected to love or guilt, care or idealism, and is an aspect of the dialogical relationships born in the possibilities of hope and change.

This book is about all of us, and, by accident or default, street kids are the conveyors of alternative perspectives on the business of our living together. I've tried to explore who street kids are, who we are, and the extent to which we intermingle in the complex geographies of the street. I've tried to illuminate the complexities that exist among and between all of us, and have attempted to highlight the values and beliefs that inform our thoughts and practices of living together. My intent was to bring an expanded vision of street kids and their lives to light by examining their narratives for what they could tell me about their values and beliefs, and by letting those values open up possibilities for new understandings and renovating ideas and questions about life on the street for kids.

Tensions and Ever More Tensions

After coming to frame what kids shared with me in the light of prophetic renewal and possibility, I wondered how these possibilities might serve as the impetus for a dialogue between the mainstream and street kids. I wondered how, given all that they had said, they could empower themselves to actualize some of the values that they foresaw in their conversations with me in a new kind of community, in a new and different life. My head started swirling; I was turning in circles, and I came upon a frightening proposition. They couldn't and probably wouldn't, and the following is an exploration into why.

There are tensions that live in between and alongside the meanings that kids make of their experiences on the street. Tensions and contradictions co-exist because life is messy and confused and confounded. The traditional literature about street kids pulls at threads of the phenomenon so that a linear, comprehensible train of thought, hypothesis, or theory can be teased out and followed from one end to the other. But for that first blush of clarity, the organic rhythm of the street is lost. The barrage of conflicted thoughts and messages, oppositional beliefs and attitudes, contested and controlled spaces and places, are ultimately absent or smoothed out, waxed like antiseptic, shiny floors that can be eaten off of until the streetscape and the streetself are reduced to entities out there, things separated from us, alien from you, from me—things that have been cleaned, and organized, and tidily conceived of and dealt with.

In extending the experience away from ourselves, someplace beyond our reach, it seems that we have forgotten to examine how it might be possible that our values, which underscore our society, precipitate or perpetuate the current climate for kids on the street. This relationship is most exquisitely exemplified by kids as they expose their perceptions of the underlying market economy values which seep into much of what we do and say, and plan, and understand.

It seems that the kids are able to talk about different values—about money, for example, as the harbinger of resentment, of hate, of love. They see it and then they see us. Money and privilege are of concern to street kids because they understand that most of us tend to chase after it, including themselves. They can name it because they see themselves as outside of it even though they engage it. And still the values that they prefer (i.e., authentic relationships, "real" friendship, non-commodified relationships of help or concern) are continually threatened and undervalued in the mainstream.

Believing in the value of helping those in need, we have convinced ourselves, because of our best intentions, that we are actively combating poverty, that we are pursuing the eradication of oppression, and that we are looking after the kids who need us. But perhaps we might question whether or not we are doing what we say we are (Carlen, 1996).

What if the ethic of the market economy is doing its job so well that it is tricking us—that is, service providers, policy planners, educators, parents, cultural theorists, and academicians—into believing that the hard work that we do is actually helpful and valuable, but that in "reality," and in terms of the market's survival, the work that we do is set up to reify and strengthen the hegemonies of the system, maintain its status quo, and constrain hope for change and possibility? How can we tell the value of what we are doing or thinking or questioning from within? Is there ever any place outside?

Ironically, the kids live in these confusions as well. They are equally muddled in a values mire. Wanting to be loved, to have community, to be judged based upon who they are, not what they are, to be respected and valued, to be heard and counted, kids articulate their oppression from beyond the borders of the mainstream. But are the places from whence they speak really situated outside the system, or are they inside but at the periphery? The kids perceive that the aforementioned aspects of being a part of a community are being withheld from them, denied them because of their homeless status. And so it is, this conflict of experience—on the one hand, receiving the negative messages about living on the street (for example, being ignored, being removed, and being reviled), and, on the other hand, finding strength and courage in surviving the circumstances of being homeless (for example, finding friends, finding community, finding self)—complicates the phenomenon of being a street kid. They aren't so sure about how to feel about their experiences on the street and are confused about how to fit in, especially, in a society whose values they don't really respect. As we have seen, they have understood something profound about the construction of our social, economic, political, and communal lives. And, they seem to be aware of how those constructions marginalize those that do not fit in, namely, themselves.

Meanwhile, although they perceive of the mainstream as the purveyor of bad values and careless living, and understand their experiences on the street as providing the fertile ground for learning something different about self and relationships, about friendship, shame, and identity—in the middle of this intense tug-of-war—street kids also know that they need to join the rank and file if they are going to find their way off the street. In other words, street kids' practical ideas about getting off the street are tied right into the system that they say they abhor. The following two examples illustrate the paradoxes that exist in street kids' feelings about the mainstream workaday world. What they perceive as their only options for improving the physical conditions of their lives seem to conflict with how they feel about "suits" and mainstream life. Crowchild shows us, in the following comments, how complex and contradictory his appreciation is for work and money.

> They [suits] care about money. They don't care much about anything else. They care about their money and they care about their jobs. They pay taxes and they pay charities because the government says they have to or whatever, right? They don't care they just want more money. More money, nice cars, big houses. Like I have a pillow and a sleeping bag, and maybe a girlfriend

every once in awhile. And I am happier than they will ever be. (Crowchild, 09/02/98)

In contrast to…

And then you have to have a place. In order to have a job, you have to have a place, but, to get a place, you have to get a job. Give me a job and let me crash at the place that I am working at least for the next little while. Until I get my paycheck and I have enough money to buy my own place or apartment. But most people won't do that because having someone sleep in the restaurant is not good for business. And that is what the business is for, to make money. The only way to make people happy is to make money. (Crowchild, 09/02/98)

Who will Crowchild be when he is one of the working folk who "don't care and just want more money"? If he is happier than "they'll ever be," what will happen to him and his happiness when he joins the mainstream? Gwen Danzig offers these opposing perspectives of what it means to work:

I wanted to get off the streets and if I could find a place to live, then I knew I could get a job and support myself. So first I went to welfare, and I said that I need an emergency check so I can get a place to live. I am tired of this; I want to get off the streets. (Gwen Danzig, 08/25/98)

Versus…

There is a lot of snobs in this city. It's overwhelming. For a city with so much wealth though, I can kind of see where half of it comes. But at the same time, I can't see why. A lot of people have this attitude that we don't look proper; we don't have the proper attitude and outlooks on life. We don't want to grow up and be blue-collar citizens that go and work eight hours a day, pay taxes, and die. (Gwen Danzig, 08/25/98)

So what will leaving the street mean to Gwen Danzig? How will he view himself if his job requires that he "work eight hours a day"?

"You know they sit there and pan and 'suits' walk by and yell 'Get a job.' They [other street kids] take it as an insult, but you know what, the 'suits' give me a slap of reality" (Neil, 11/12/98). The "slap of reality" to which Neil refers seems to me to be about our world being defined by employment ideals. I can't help but wonder about the confusions that must arise as a result of learning or feeling or seeing flaws in the construction of our monied world, and at the same time knowing that this is the world that awaits their participation after the street. What must that feel like? Grub told me that he'll "appreciate things that [he's] got like a house, food, and things like that a lot more than [he] did before because [he's] lived without a lot of stuff for a long time and it sucks" (Grub, 11/02/98). I can hear the relief in what Grub is telling me about being away from the harsh experiences of the street, but I can't help wonder what might be lost in making the journey from the margins to the mainstream.

Like little sparks extinguishing one by one, street kids' have limited options because "we" have not conceived of making change for them that doesn't involve joining the mainstream. And, although they have visioned a different world with different values, they are equally disempowered to make these changes because they lack the resources to "buy themselves out."

Yet reading the literature, engaging in this research, philosophizing about the meanings of marginal voices from beyond the parameters of the mainstream, writing this book, and listening to kids tell their stories about their lives on the street, would suggest to me that the street kid issue is a central concern to many of us. Given that street kids are occupying a larger space in the public imagination, given that there is a significant amount of research on the subject, given that governments are also paying attention to the existence of street kids on their streets and in their public spaces, I am left wondering why the numbers of street kids are steadily increasing (Community and Neighbourhood Services, 1998). We deliberate on how or why kids come to the street, and from these musings, we try to figure out how we can help, that is, how we can get kids off the street. But maybe we are asking the wrong questions, or rather, perhaps our questions are only reflective of a singular vision of what it means to be a street kid and what the solution to that problem is, or could be. We've organized to look after impoverished kids and other marginalized and outcast members of society. Yet, have we not also become complicit in systems that (as we have explored in this text) appear to delimit kids' freedoms on the street, and attempt to erase them from the landscape?

Technological rationality and lining up all our ducks. In another huge hermeneutic spiral, questioning the ontological and epistemological boundaries of systems and their freedoms, constraints, effects, and opportunities, I came to realize that our North American, globalized operating system is more pervasive than I had hoped. As I mentioned in Chapter Two, "we have committed a grave sin." That sin is more drastic, more pervasive, and more elusive than I had originally imagined. Initially, I was awakened to the realization that service providers, among others, were complicit in maintaining poverty, homelessness, and marginalization (Carlen, 1996). This understanding came to me as a result of the experience of being deflected from the agencies with whom I wanted to connect to initiate this research. But I wasn't able to account for why. I understand now that service providers, government workers, etc., are not complicit in maintaining the status quo because they are evil, or have bad values, or don't really care about the people with whom they work, but, rather, because care has been organized in certain ways beyond their control and architecture.

> Marcuse depicts a situation in which there are no revolutionary classes or groups to militate for radical social change and in which individuals are integrated into the existing society, content with their lot and unable to perceive possibilities for a happier and freer life. (Kellner, 1991, cited in Marcuse, 1964, xxix)

I became aware of the extent to which the tacit contracts which dictate our social living arrangements help to maintain the status quo. That was clearer to me in terms of the influence of market-driven values affecting services, budgets, and policies. But that first realization was only the beginning of what has now emerged as a much more problematic proposition.

Throughout my conversations with street kids, they outlined, addressed, and articulated the extent to which everything is stacked against them, how they are set outside of the dominant culture, and how they are judged harshly for that. I've tried to piece together the meanings that they make of their lives, connecting their interpretations with mine, and ours with yours. Groping for new meanings and alternative perspectives on street kids and society, imagining how we all intersect in this phenomenon, I landed in a different place. I see something bigger now, something more hopeful and more philosophic than I anticipated.

In a technologically rational society (Marcuse, 1964), all the ducks are lined up to accommodate the hegemonic ideology—in this case, that would be to create material wealth, to accumulate power, to have comfort, to be employed, to be "normal." Street kids, the poor, and the needy are therefore seen as imperfections in the technologically rational plan. Perturbations in the otherwise "rational" system need to be attended to so as to further the survival of the system. In this case, we have agreed that the instrumental tasks of caring for each other will be handled by the agencies and other institutions to look after these "glitches" in our system. But this seems to be only part of the problem.

It seems that the dominant ideology has so efficiently taught us about our society and culture, has so effectively convinced us that street kids are manifestations of the failures of our otherwise effective operating ideology, that the vista through which we can conceive of this phenomenon is severely and terminally limited. In other words, street kids have not been successfully "rationalized" yet, and it is in that vein that we interpret all that happens on the street and all that kids say about it.

> ...the consumer society and the apparatus of planning and management in advanced capitalism had produced new forms of social administration and a "society without opposition" that threatened individuality and that closed off possibilities of radical social change. (Kellner, 1991, cited in Marcuse, 1964, xxv)

The ironic thing is that street kids are equally caught up in the hegemony of the social and philosophical order. In that light, street kids can only envision their instrumental escape from the street by joining the dominant culture—finding work, accumulating goods, transforming into "suits," even well-intentioned "suits." I asked Gwen Danzig what becomes of street kids when they get older? He paused and thought and then replied, "They disappear" (08/24/98).

I wonder if Gwen Danzig was telling me something about how the contested spaces that kids inhabit on the street get fused into the mainstream over time. Maybe he was telling me that the street as a site of kids' resilience and resistance can only endure for so long before the force of the "technologically rational" world sucks them into its gargantuan belly. Maybe he was saying that whatever alternatives for social and communal living street kids come to know through their experiences there, the only real choice for them is that they have to give up and join in. In this light, I understood something new about the profundity of what Gwen Danzig said when he told me that "[we've] turned ourselves into tools basically. We are no longer people. We are just tools and numbers" (Gwen Danzig, 08/25/98).

I didn't realize it at the time, but this is a part of what I was hearing all along. Mike alluded to it in his comments about the divisions between the sane and the insane. He said:

> People operate in all sorts of different manners and because somebody doesn't operate the way that most people operate, makes them crazy. I think that's stupid, and I think because somebody doesn't fit in properly and they don't act the same, that gives someone else the right to lock them up and dope them up on all sorts of drugs. (Mike, 10/29/98)

Not fitting in is precisely what Marcuse (1964) suggests the hegemonies of the time try to eradicate. "Hence to dissent from liberal modernity is to fall silent, for we have no terms in which to speak that do not issue from the very space we are trying to speak against" (Lee, 1998, 16). This meant an entirely new thing to me and had also broadened how I might question kids' agency and docility in their lives in the contested spaces of the street.

And so I felt that I had come to a place where I thought I understood a little more about the kids' lives on the street and the connections of those lives to both the systems that intersect with the kids and perhaps also the philosophical organization of those systems in perpetuating their survival. It dawned on me that maybe we are severed from alternative modes of thinking because we've stopped straining to hear what is barely even audible (Heschel, 1962) and are trapped in a system that is effectively "atrophying the very possibilities of radical social change and human emancipation" (Kellner, 1991, cited in Marcuse, 1964, xxix).

As parents and teachers, as therapists and citizens, we want our kids to have dreams; we ourselves want to actualize; we count on freedom being a mainstay of our Western culture and believe that "you can be whatever you want to be," but what are the possibilities for these "truisms" to become manifest? Do you remember what your dreams were? Did you imagine a more just social order when you were younger? Could you see the flaws and inequalities in our system, and did you believe that you would do something about them when you got older? Did you? The lasting tension with which I am now confronted is: If this is what we are trapped in, how are we going to get out?

If You Name It, You'll Be Free: Peace and Possibilities

The dilemma presented above is both startling, frightening, and exhilarating. How much bigger could the "boogie-man" get? But in actuality, entertaining the possibility that we are veiled by the hegemonies of our time has been the most liberating concept I've encountered thus far. Marcuse (1964) opens the door for renewal and revision, for possibilities and change that otherwise might have been difficult for me to imagine. That is to say, after learning about street kids' lives and connecting those lives to the sociopolitical and economic fabric of our shared lives, I might have worked myself into a dark and dank place where no options and no hope are possible. The opposite has occurred.

> It may be the meaning and place of children in our lives is the most important consideration to be taken up...not just because the voice of the young has been translated out of any meaningful involvement with the powers that be, but also because the question of the young (their conception, care, and nurturance) devolves precisely on so many of the defining issues of our time, such as the meaning of power, gender relations, and the matter of how we might learn to live more responsibly within the earthly web of our planetary home. (Smith, 1994, 102)

Maybe if we name the things that constrain us, we can work toward changing the conditions of our lives, reaffirming the values to which we want to ascribe, and reconnecting with the moral practices that might guide our everyday activities. The kids have already started showing me the way. Grant (1995) suggests that people cannot simply choose to accept or reject the mass cultures in which they live. He concludes that "only by constant and relentless reflection on this modern idea [i.e., the instrumentalist view of reason, dominance, and capitalism] can we hope to liberate ourselves from the naïve acceptance of it" (11). Such reflection has been the inertia of this inquiry and the focus of this book. Lee (1998) suggests that "[w]e meditate with our whole lives: with our passions and mind and our past and our deepest hungers" (55). And so I've tried to meditate on the lives of street kids, on my life, and on the lives that we share together on this planet, in the hope of understanding something new about street kids and positively affecting all of our lives.

"Young people have not been enfranchised by the research conducted on their lives" (Valentine, Skelton, & Chambers, 1998, 21). I have tried, in my research, to hear them, to listen to them, and to meet them in their terrain. With "good will" (Gadamer, 1989 cited in Risser, 1997, 167, see Chapter Three), I've tried to bring a renewed understanding to bear on street kids' lives and have grappled with and reflected on the meanings of those lives as they've directed and connected me to places beyond my horizons. I have endeavored, through the issues and tensions expressed throughout this text, to open some of the multiple dialogues that may continue to inform us as we revision ourselves and our world. It is my hope that by recasting how we take up, listen to, think about, and engage with street kids and each other, we will be strengthened to continue our individual and collective struggles for meaning, hope, possibility, and peace.

Chapter Seven

Epilogue

So now that we've been to the street and back, and now that we've explored some of the issues that confront and affront street kids, now that we've travelled to the locales where identities get forged in the sociopolitical entanglings of the streetscape, and now that we've recast our understanding of street kids' agency and docility as they are mingled with our own actions and inactions, and now that we have explored the complex of systems rooted in the fabric of street kids' lives, we are summoned, again, to question how we've been—and how we are—a part of that complicated topography. We needn't have been confrontative with a street kid nor have intended any harm. We may, in fact, be kind, caring, and gentle people—people with the best of intentions—but we are, nonetheless, co-architects of a system that creates, maintains, and abides marginalized and oppressed kids. Questions about how we might untangle ourselves from the systems that rely and require our compliance are too complex to answer with suggestions for alternative practices and prescriptions for innovative social service or educational programming. That, it seems to me, has been one of the problems all along. We've been too interested in the bottom line; we've been too interested in answers that can give us instructions for how we might make change to accommodate whatever we have taken up from this text and others. But in spite of our inclinations to "wrap things up" and minimize contradictions and ambiguities in favor of clarity and direction, I've intended this book to leave us entirely someplace else. My desire has been to raise questions, to cause discomfort, to shake and cajole us out of our malignant complacency. My aim has been to unearth the embodied ethos that lives deep in the recesses of who we are and to raise it up in order to examine its impact on how we live in relationship with ourselves, with each other, with "others" who we name as "other," and with our planet. What are we doing and why? How are we treating each other and our kids within our various communities? What effects do dominant ideologies have on the ways we are called to "be" with each other in the myriad places and spaces that we inhabit together? To these ends, no superficial implications can be uttered, because we must, in the still, quiet moments of our reflection, live with street kids' words and allow them to penetrate our undeniable resistances.

This book began with an invitation for reading. I didn't realize then that the invitation that I made those many pages ago extends beyond how I invited you to read my work—hermeneutically, pedagogically, and critically. That invitation is also about the future. It's about how we might take away meanings and ideas about street kids, how we might think about streetscapes, how we might look with eyes anew at panhandling kids, how public space might come alive in our consideration as that which represents a complex of ideological constructs conflicting in the landscape of the street, and how we might re-vision our work as parents, educators, citizens, scholars, kids, psychologists, professionals, or human beings.

I didn't realize those years ago how this work would change me, how it would affect what I see and what I ask, how I would be called to it well beyond the parameters of my academic life. Being with kids on the street, listening to what they told me, and taking up the uncomfortable topic of homelessness for kids was a most profound experience. Connecting with them as I travelled the streets in my painted t-shirt compelled me to find a way to make meaning of my own life, as street kids implicated me in their narratives and captured me in our shared social web. This experience was and is a gift. My eyes are open in new ways, in ways that are also always changing, in ways that call me to unearth what would be so much more bearable if left to lie dormant, silent, and entombed.

Appendix I

Re-reading Street Kids

The literature on street kids is vast and varied, perhaps even as much as are the lives of street kids. This body of literature contributed to my understanding of street kids[14] and helped me conceptualize where street kids are located in academic discourses. Although this literature does not pertain directly to the substantive topic of this book (i.e., panhandling, politics, and place as the embodiment of street kids' conditions and experiences on the street), I believe that these data provide the background to some of the questions that I have asked about research, street kids, marginalization, and oppression.

This body of research exemplifies for me the kind of fragmentation and compartmentalization that is pervasive in traditional treatments of street kids in scholarly research. By conversing with these data and questioning the data for potential blind spots, I discovered that the way we take up a topic, the mind-set that informs our practice, the perspective from which our questions and curiosities develop, the nature of our conceptions about how we might or might not be able to separate ideas and events, and the consequences thereof, significantly impact the kind of research that we do.

And so, the possibility for learning that flowed from my reading of this literature led me to look anew at street kids, led me to be a skeptic, carefully questioning and investigating the academic discourses for what

---

[14] Please note that this review is based on literature from industrialized nations and may not pertain to street kids experiences in developing countries or countries affected by civil unrest or war.

they were and weren't telling me. In retrospect, I understand that this literature impelled me to look deeper into the lives of street kids. My reading directed me on this path, urged me to evaluate the meanings and connections that tie together the literature with lived experiences, and ideologies with interruptions. What follows is a review of the literature as it was experienced in helping me frame my understandings of street kids.

In reading the literature I became frustrated, angry, and dissatisfied. I was looking for information that would deliver a profound understanding of what was going on for kids on the street. I was looking to expand my understanding of street kids and the dynamics of street life so that I would/could be a better practitioner, a better helper, a more informed scholar, and an active and concerned citizen. I found the literature had two fundamental problems. First, there seemed to be a number of issues missing from the literature, and second, the literature appeared to be quite fragmented. As a result of these two different but interrelated problems, it was difficult to understand what living a street kid's life is like. It strikes me that the literature has become splintered because research has tended to explicate the separate components of street life. For example, some research looks at the variety of types of street kids (e.g., those who run away, those who are thrown out, and those who are seeking adventure). Whereas other research focuses on the familial or causal conditions that initiated the running behavior (e.g., sexual abuse, physical abuse, emotional abuse, neglect, discord with parents, and financial strain). And a third group of research investigates issues or behaviors that are prevalent on the street itself (e.g., prostitution, drug use and abuse, criminal behavior, sexual beliefs and behavior, and suicide). Although this list is not exhaustive, it illustrates the compartmentalization that has resulted in the focused nature of research initiatives with street kids. In an effort to understand the diversity of the street kid population as well as to get some understanding of the mélange of issues prevalent for street kids, things have been presented in a piecemeal fashion. Few studies investigate the phenomenon as it is lived.[15]

In the next section I will attempt to piece together the fragments of

---

[15] See, for example, Carlen, 1996; Hagan & McCarthy, 1997; Lundy, 1995; Plympton, 1997.

information from the literature by re-connecting the causal and interrelated factors of street youth and their lives from what I have found in the literature. This review follows, to some degree, the path that previous studies have undertaken, to the detriment of our ability to understand the complexity and totality of the phenomenon and of street kids' lives.

What the Literature Does and Does Not Say

Issues that confront street youth before leaving home are reported to be manifold. They include: (a) family relationships, including parental conflict,[16] (b) sexual abuse,[17] and (c) physical or emotional abuse.[18] Research that investigates the street kid phenomenon has focused primarily on who street kids are and what kind of backgrounds they come from. These studies have elucidated to some degree the potential profile of a street kid. In other words, the literature can answer questions regarding the kinds of families street kids tend to come from. When I asked such questions as what is living on the street like for adolescents, how are the lives of street kids structured, or how do street kids structure their lives, the literature was virtually silent. There is only minimal discussion of what the life of a street kid might be like, what it feels like to be homeless, or to be a runaway, or throwaway, or to be marginalized.[19] What do streets kid see? What experiences in their lives are meaningful to them? How do they perceive society? How do they perceive themselves? Of what are they afraid? How do they perceive fear? What about street life inspires fear? Are

---

[16] See Bradley, 1997; Dadds, Braddock, Cuers, & Elliot, 1993; De Man, Dolan, Pelletier, & Reid, 1993, 1994; Ek & Steelman, 1988; Hagan & McCarthy, 1997; Hier, Korboot, & Schweitzer, 1990; Kufeldt, Durieux, Nimmo, & McDonald, 1992; Kurtz, Jarvis, & Kurtz, 1991; Kurtz, Kurtz, & Jarvis, 1991; Russell, 1998; Schweitzer & Hier, 1993; Schweitzer, Hier, & Terry, 1994; Stefanidis, Pennbridge, MacKenzie, & Pottharst, 1992.

[17] See Caputo, Weiler, & Kelly, 1994a, 1994b; Famularo, Kinscherff, Fenton, & Bolduc, 1990; Janus, Burgess, & McCormack, 1987; Kufeldt & Nimmo, 1987a; Kufeldt & Nimmo, 1987b; Kurtz, Jarvis, & Kurtz, 1991; Kurtz, Kurtz, & Jarvis, 1991; McCormack, Janus, & Burgess, 1986; Russell, 1998; Warren, Gary, & Moorhead, 1994.

[18] See Carlson, 1991; Famularo et al., 1990; Feitel, Margetson, Chamas, & Lipman, 1992; Powers, Eckenrode, & Jaklitsch, 1990; Russell, 1998; Warren et al., 1994.

[19] For exceptions, see Carlen, 1996; Hagan & McCarthy, 1997; Lundy, 1995; Ruddick, 1996.

they better off emotionally on the street than they would be elsewhere? Why? These are only a few of the questions that emerged as I inquired about issues around homeless youth and their lived experiences.

The fact that these questions are not adequately answered does not mean that the literature does not illuminate certain aspects of the street kids phenomenon. I think that whatever is missing from the literature base (i.e., that which records the experiences of young people living on the street as well as that which translates those narratives into understanding the fabric of our lives) has been overlooked, or ignored because of a lack of in-depth studies that focus on street youth and the complexities of their lives. There is an audible silence in the literature; little is known or understood about youth who make their way to the street and what that path may look like or consist of. What steps are involved in becoming entrenched in street culture? It seems until recently the academic literature has kept the stories and experiences of street kids at bay, perhaps in an effort to avoid the painful issues that surround this phenomenon, or perhaps because the research methods most often used have no place for stories. What I found most disturbing about the majority of the literature was the apparent lack of humanity in these scholarly works. A number of questions emerged as I read the literature, the most pressing of which pertained to the conditions in which young people find themselves on the street and the meaning they ascribe to those circumstances. Since I had the experience of working on the street, I felt that I had at least some understanding of the issues that confronted street kids.

In reading the literature, I was constantly comparing what I had learned from working on the street with what I was reading in the literature. I searched for what I had thought to be the salient, pressing, urgent, scary, and destructive experiences of street life for kids in the literature. For example, I believe that a current trend for young women on the street is to become pregnant purposefully. Still, I couldn't find much information to expand on the reasons why young women want to have babies. Questions about the meaningfulness of having children or of becoming a parent seemed to be absent. There was no information about the intent of the pregnancy or potential gain these young women were anticipating. I wondered whether there was a reason for the research to be silent about something that seems so critical. I was perplexed at the gap between the academic representation of street life and the lived reality of it (as I understood it from my work experience). I plodded on, however, trying to uncover research that seemed to reflect what actually goes on on the street. Almost to no avail.

Literature Format

As I delved into the vast sea of literature covering street life and street kids, I began to notice a particular formula for the delivery of the information. Something was bothering me as I moved through the literature. I puzzled over what it could be and then realized it was the language. It seems that the language used to describe, explicate, and inform this phenomenon is pristine, sterile, organized, clear, cold, and removed. There is no sense of immediacy transmitted to the reader; there is no sense of immediacy related to the youth about whom this literature speaks. Odd, because there seemed to me to be a tremendous sense of immediacy on the street, and life on the street is neither neat nor pristine. Language, I realized, had been used only as a way of putting information on paper as opposed to being a conduit through which the dialogic experience could be initiated between reader and writer. In other words, the data are reported, but the writing appears severed from the lifeworld of the topic. In many cases, the language had been "cleaned up" to the point that I had difficulty recognizing it to be about the lives that are at risk on the street, about the people with whom I had come into contact. For example, this is how a street kid described the events precipitating leaving home (quoted from a non-academic, service delivery source):

> My aunt kicked me out 'cause we got in an argument over a birthday gift that I bought for my cousin. She started bringing up my past and threatened to send me back to my adoptive family who sexually abused me. She told me to get out the next day. I left, went to school and never went back. (Female, seventeen- year-old, homeless, cited in Radford, King, & Warren, 1991)

This reveals a number of things about this young woman who is recalling how she came to be on the street. The academic literature, on the other hand, reports the conditions precipitating leaving home in an altogether different manner. For example, "Parent-youth conflict, physical abuse, and school problems continue to emerge as situational variables which are associated with adolescent runaway behaviour" (Roberts, 1982, cited in Radford et al., 1991). In the severed, impersonal, academic version, the reasons for leaving home leave little room for personal biography, for perspective, for voice, or for personhood. This is but one example which illuminates the chasm between the thick descriptions of the experience as they are given by street kids, and the removed, severed-sounding generalizations given by the academe.

What this taught me about writing and reading, and about the problems that I was noticing in the literature, is that language (especially in the writing up of research data) represents something more than the words which appear on paper. Language itself is more than the words it speaks. It transmits feeling, conviction; it conveys a message; it is the gestalt of the information being delivered coupled with the voice of the writer and the voices and textures of the characters and contexts. It is the linkage we have to understanding something new about the thoughts and feelings of another. Even though we can never mirror in language the fullest extent of experience (Gadamer, 1995) and although all narratives are interpretations of experience (Britzman, 1991; Gadamer, 1995; Gallagher, 1992; Jardine, 1992, 1998; Smith, 1994), it is the way we communicate with each other and must be valued for its richness, its diversity, and its ability to open up discourses between people and issues. Whatever language street kids use, seems to me, to be invaluable for identifying what is meaningful for them in their lives. Unfortunately, I had noticed that the language which kids use to talk about their lives gets filtered out when researchers write articles about them. Their words are all but amputated from them when they are studied and when the language that they use to describe, explicate, or communicate their lived experiences gets translated into statistics, prevalence rates, or percentages.

Thus far, I have attempted to explain two issues related to the literature on street kids that I took notice of, that I believed to be salient insofar as understanding what and how the literature is informing on the street kid phenomenon. The first was an examination of the disparity in the literature with regard to what the lived reality of the street is from my point of view, and the second was a more "technical" glance at the way in which the literature has been written. These next sections explore what the literature offers about the street kid phenomenon, and, conversely, what it does not.

Defining Street Kids

Delineations between types of street kids are plentiful in the literature. In fact, most of the scholarship on the topic of street kids begins by defining who these kids are and how or why they have come to the street. Street youth are most commonly referred to in the literature as runaways or throwaways, reinforcing the notion that many are escaping domestic crises. Typically, two factors define runaway youth: (a) their young age; and (b) absence from home without a parent's permission, usually for 24 hours or more (Shane, 1996). In the case of throwaways, the second criterion does not apply; parents of these adolescents overtly reject their children (Colby, 1990; Hurwitz, & Hurwitz, 1997). There are, however, a number of additional definitions used to describe the adolescent living on the street. Generally, these definitions attempt to capture the specifics around how these youth got to the street and/or the characteristics of what they have left behind. Examples of other definitions include: (a) curb-siders, youth living on the street part time (Brannigan & Caputo, 1993; Zide & Cherry, 1992); (b) runners from care, youth who have run from institutions (Bradley, 1997; Miller, Eggertson-Tacon, & Quigg, 1990); and (c) forsaken, youth who have left home because of economic strife in the family (Lundy, 1995; Zide & Cherry, 1992).

Definitional distinctions have been researched in an effort to depict the multiplicity of causes (or consequences) which bring children to the street. These distinctions are in no way exhaustive, nor are they mutually exclusive (Brannigan & Caputo, 1993). Colby (1990) argues that such distinctions are crucial in order to plan and provide services which adequately meet the needs of sub-sections of this heterogeneous group (Daly, 1998). Unfortunately, to add to the difficulty imbedded in the definitional web of constructs, these distinctions often go the way of the window when a specific issue is being researched. For example, studies that investigate HIV risk behavior on the street generally do not delineate between the kinds of street kids involved as participants. To this end, we might ask what the relevance of the distinctions is if they are not used in and across research topics. On the other hand, definitional distinctions do expand the scope of understanding people can glean from reading the research. So I asked, does this information lend itself to understanding the phenomenon of living a street kid's life? Partially. The literature tells me something about the conditions from which street kids emerge. However, knowing whether a street kid was thrown out or ran away seemed insufficient in transmitting to me the totality of their lived experiences, and, specifically, it left me wanting to know more about how kids come to the street.[20]

Typologies

Typologies of street kids have been offered in an attempt to aid in the classification and comprehension of street kids' movement from their place of residence to the street. Two kinds of research have typically been undertaken to elucidate this phenomenon. The first includes studies which represent risk factors associated with high-risk or running behavior evidenced among youth who are living at home or who are living in residential care (Kashubeck, Pottebaum, & Read, 1994; McWhirter, McWhirter, McWhirter & McWhirter, 1994). The vast majority of typological research, however, emanates from studies that investigate street youth, and then, based upon the information gathered from these studies, classification systems of street youth are developed. There are distinctions in the kinds of typologies put forward. There are classification systems which describe definitional distinctions within the street youth population (Jones, 1988; Zide & Cherry, 1992). A second kind of typology involves the description of the processes of running away (Ek & Steelman, 1988; Palenski & Launer, 1987). And lastly, a third kind of typology describes the various kinds of paradigms in which street youth are investigated (e.g.,

---

[20] It is important to note that throwaways are almost a non-entity in the literature. The literature is primarily focused on running away.

psychosocial, pathological, delinquent, etc.) (Csapo, 1987; Van der Ploeg, 1989).

Antecedents

For many youth the flight from home involves a process that leads to the ultimate end point of the street. One view of that process involves parental-child discord, and a breaking point at which time the situation becomes intolerable either for the parent or for the child. Ek and Steelman (1988) report that the process underlying the decision to run away involves a critical incident between parent and child and a final decision to leave. They suggest that this process may involve parents threatening their children and perhaps inspiring the decision to leave. Additionally, Ek and Steelman (1988) report a three-tiered process of running away. The components include (a) managing the fear around leaving home, (b) planning the logistics and timing of the run, and (c) actually leaving home or not returning home in the case of the adolescent who leaves from school or elsewhere.

Palenski and Launer (1987) provide a different perspective on the process of youth getting to the street. They propose a typology which describes the transition of youth from place of residence to the street by examining the behaviors and attitudes which must be mastered in order for a youth to survive on the street. They propose that a "runner identity" is developed upon the successful completion of certain tasks, attitudinal changes, and coping responses. The fundamental components related to the transition onto the street include (a) managing residual feelings about home, (b) managing self on the street and providing oneself with basic needs (i.e., food, shelter, etc.), (c) engaging in street behavior to facilitate full transition to the street (e.g., petty theft, prostitution, drug use, etc.), and (d) "making it" on the street which is related to the quality of life the adolescent experiences once on the street. It has also been purported that those youth with the least to lose (i.e., conflictual or abusive family relationships) are the most likely to run away and stay away (Whitbeck & Simons, 1990).

The two examples of transitional typologies may provide a partial picture of what adolescents live through as they make their way onto the street. As I read this literature, my understanding of the processes involved in leaving home was supplemented to some degree. But in the volumes that have been written on street youth, these are some of the only examples of research that attempt to describe the process of running away from home. Much to my amazement, I could not find research that investigated any psychological ramifications around the decision-making process for running, nor about how kids were feeling about leaving their places of residence. Issues like being frightened, feeling lost, not knowing where to go, feeling ashamed, or angry, surprisingly did not seem to be components that were included when developing typologies of running behavior. These typological exemplars seem to be little more than additional classification systems although they do shed additional light on the topic. And further, it's been over a decade since these typologies were offered, and literature reviews continue to cite these same studies (for example, in Russell, 1998). The question that beckons is why, after so long, are these still the typologies to which we refer?

What I found to be wanting from the typological literature was a more profound investigation of what it means for a kid to make the decision to leave home. I am still asking: What are the psychological, emotional, or affective processes involved with getting to the street? What was different about the incident that inspired the flight from home than previous fights? What meaning did kids ascribe to the whole concept of "running away;" does the term carry any baggage of its own? Does leaving home suggest certain things about a kid?

Causal Factors

What makes children leave home? Much of the research indicates that many youth on the street are fleeing from destructive homes, homes characterized by abuse, neglect, and violence. It is hypothesized that children leave home because they want to exert their independence, they are looking for adventure, they don't share common values with their parents, because of issues around sexual orientation, because they don't want to take responsibility for their actions, and/or a host of other explanations. There are a number of studies, however, which support the contention that most runaway street youth are running from something, not running to something (Csapo, 1987; Whitbeck & Simons, 1990). This kind of inquiry represents a major part of the research initiative undertaken with these kids.

Overwhelmingly, street youth report that their homes (including foster care) are fraught with conflictual relationships with parents, sexual, physical and/or emotional abuse, including neglect and violence (Bradley, 1997; Carlson, 1991; Janus et al.,1987; Kufeldt & Nimmo, 1987a, 1987b; Kurtz, Kurtz, & Jarvis, 1991; McCormack et al., 1986; Powers et al., 1990; Radford et al., 1991; Rimsza, Berg, & Locke, 1988; Russell, 1998; Warren et al., 1994; Whitbeck & Simons, 1990). I was not surprised by these findings, but I began to wonder what makes one abused kid leave home while another does not. I cannot help wondering about whether or not the question of selfhood or identity is the motivation for leaving. It seems to me that issues concerning "self" are critical and perhaps more pronounced for kids on the street, kids who have had to exert themselves or save themselves from destructive environments. Or alternatively, perhaps the street is the training ground most appealing for attaining an identity (Hetherington, 1998). What does it mean to be a street kid anyway, and how does that affect the self? Interestingly, Bradley (1997) found that homeless youth in New York exhibited less depression and higher self-esteem than other kids had shown in similar studies. Homeless kids' results compared similarly to levels of self-esteem in their non-homeless contemporaries. What does that mean about kids finding their way to the street? Does the street become the place for personal pedagogy, for learning about oneself and about the world? What does that mean for kids?

Parental conflict. Research indicates that a major factor associated with young people's decision to leave home is conflictual parent-child relationships including parental control, violence in the home, perceived parental indifference to the child, and being afraid of parents when in trouble (Bradley, 1997; Hagan & McCarthy, 1997; Russell, 1998; Whitbeck & Simons, 1990). In a large-scale comparison between teenage runaways and non-runaways (Loeb, Burke, & Boglarsky, 1986), findings indicate that for runaways, conflict with parents included differences in values, a need for independence, and issues of parental control. From reading studies such as this, it became clearer to me that meanings and values play a significant role in initiating a kid's flight from home. Although this seems a viable explanation for running, threats of violence or being in trouble with parents are not frequently cited in the literature as a reason for leaving home.

Except for Whitbeck and Simons' (1990) investigation of victimization of homeless and runaway adolescents which uses "in trouble and afraid to go home" (116) as a reason for running away, and Janus, Archambault, Brown, and Welsh's (1995) survey of physical abuse among Canadian runaways which included "threatened with a weapon" (439) as a catalyst for running, fear of and potential for violence are not included among the general cohorts of reasons for running. In other studies which look at the response of running away as a result of familial conflict, it is posited (Miller et al., 1990) that the flight from home is often a reactive response to stress and conflict and based on irrational beliefs. Whether the beliefs are realistic or not seems less relevant than the significance of the perceived fear situation on the part of the kid who then makes the decision to leave.

There seems to be support for that contention in the literature. Radford et al. (1991) concluded that ongoing interpersonal conflict with parents was cited by throwaways to be the most common reason for leaving. Adams, Gullota, and Clancy (1985) examined the similarities and differences between runaways and throwaways. This study found that 74 percent of the runaways reported leaving home because they were not getting along with parents, and 84 percent of throwaways reported difficulties with parents as the primary reason for leaving. More recently, Lundy (1995) also concluded that the homeless kids she interviewed cited parental discord as a common reason for being on the street. After reading these data, I am left wanting to know more about their values, more about the meanings they ascribe to their lives. Here again the question of identity surfaces, and I am wanting to understand what street kids' senses of themselves are like and how they come to be?

Attachment and street kids. It seems that the literature, in the main, identifies conflict with parents as a primary reason for kids' leaving home. Few studies look at the causal constructs of coming to the street from a more theoretical standpoint. One of the few theoretical approaches to understanding how and why kids end up on the street might be found in recent research that looks at the phenomenon through a more developmental framework. In an effort to connect and collect salient causal concepts pertaining to kids who make their way to the street, attachment theory (Bowlby, 1969, cited in Schweitzer et al, 1994) will be reviewed outlining how this approach may help to explain why some kids run and some do not.

In a discussion on adolescent development, Violato and Travis (1994) identified a number of tasks which face the adolescent. When "the standards and paths of childhood are [now] inappropriate, [and] adult alternatives are untried, unhoned, and frequently not allowed or unavailable" (32), adolescents are confronted with the critical questions of how to act, who they are, what they are supposed to think and feel, and so on. An important question which these authors raised is "[h]ow does one prepare for life apart from one's family of origin?" (32).

There is an underlying assumption being put forward that separation and individuation from one's family of origin comes at an expected time, that this process is a rite of passage that ultimately enables adolescents to prepare for this eventuality (Powers & Jaklitsch, 1993). But what about the street kid who has not had this experience—whose developmental trajectory has been disturbed? Assessing why some kids run to the street and others do not is more than just acknowledging why they left home, which seems to be the approach taken by most of the literature. That is to say, many kids are sexually abused but only some of them end up on the street.

Schweitzer et al. (1994) investigated how homeless and non-homeless adolescents perceived parental care. The study reported that homeless kids perceived their parents as less caring than did non-homeless kids. This finding is consistent with Bowlby's (1969 cited in Schweitzer, et. al., 1994) assertion that "low levels of parental care are associated with weak bonding" (44). Additionally, poor attachment may lead children to resent and/or fear attachment to adults, thereby creating a situation in which significant difficulties are evidenced when kids are trying to meet their needs on the street (Powers & Jaklitsch, 1993). This may have implications for understanding street kids. Alexander (1992) found that adult attachment and long-term effects of child sexual abuse are correlationally related, and although research between the two areas is limited (the effects of sexual abuse are beyond the scope of this review), attachment theory may provide a good conceptual framework for understanding adolescent running behavior.

Stefanidis et al. (1992) examined youth readiness to move from the street to a more stable living environment. Results indicate that those kids who were "stabilization non-responsive," meaning that they left the program prematurely or did not comply with the procedures, had significantly lower attachment history as assessed by the Attachment History Questionnaire. The ramifications of having poor attachment (either insecure or avoidant) may play a role in why some kids stay away from home or why some kids maintain their lives on the street. Whichever the case, it would be interesting to investigate how attachment to primary care-givers in early life mitigates running-away behavior in adolescence. Plass and Hotaling (1995) posited that homelessness among adolescents may be intergenerationally linked. These authors examined intergenerational running patterns among runaways and their parents and found that 24 percent of the parents had run away when they were kids. Although the findings in this study do not illuminate if and how the transgenerational running response is handed down from parent to child, it does point researchers in the direction of attachment issues both in the family of origin of the parent, and in the family in which the parent is the primary care-giver of the current runaway.

Sexual abuse. Two distinctions are prevalent in the literature on sexual abuse among street youth. One is related to the reasons street youth cite for leaving home, and the second is related to the experiences street youth report having while living at home. Stiffman (1989b) cautions that many youth do not report sexual abuse as the reason for leaving home but have been sexually abused. The prevalence of sexual abuse among street youth is reported to be as high as 73 percent among adolescent females and 38 percent among adolescent males (Whitbeck & Simons, 1990). So what the literature is telling me is that the majority of kids on the street may have suffered sexual abuse while living in their homes. What I found particularly interesting is that although many youth report having been sexually abused, there is a disparity between reports that cite sexual abuse as the reason for leaving. Kufeldt and Nimmo (1987b) report that only 7 percent of respondents cited sexual abuse as the primary reason for leaving; Caputo et al. (1994b) found that 25 percent of kids cite sexual abuse as the primary reason for leaving, and Russell (1998) reports that 50 percent of her sample reported maltreatment as the reason for leaving. Here again, I am tempted to ask why some abused kids are inspired to leave home while others are not. While Russell (1998) does not specifically answer that question, she found that sexual abuse coupled with whether or not kids had left home on their own mitigated psychological distress. Kids who externalized their distress (e.g., robbing or lying) had been told to leave, whereas those kids who internalized their distress had left home on their own. What will we make of that? Russell (1998) concluded that some of her results were inexplicable because exposure to sexual assault, alcohol abuse, symptoms of depression, and a history of suicide were found in kids who measured higher levels of self-esteem than those who showed the opposite. I wonder if those kids who demonstrate more symptomatology are the same kids who have a fighting and enduring sense of self, an internal strength that hasn't been accounted for in the melee of constructs around sexual abuse and being on the street.

Physical abuse. Studies have demonstrated that one reason why young people leave their homes is due to violence. Kurtz, Kurtz, and Jarvis (1991) found that of 2,019 runaway respondents, 27 percent reported some kind of abuse at home prior to running away. Physical abuse was reported 16.8 percent of the time, as compared to 5.4 percent for sexual abuse, and 5.5 percent for both physical and sexual abuse combined. Warren et al. (1994) reported 66.7 percent of 78 respondents reported some type of abuse at home, with 30.3 percent specifying physical abuse. Russell (1998) reported that 79.3 percent of homeless kids disclosed history of physical assault.

The causal factors herein discussed do not represent all street youth but, rather, common elements in family histories among the population in question. It is difficult to obtain an accurate depiction as to why some adolescents run and others do not. The samples used in the aforementioned studies represent street youth who have volunteered to fill out self-report questionnaires or engage in interviews which are often conducted in shelters and other facilities servicing this population. But there are adolescents who may not come into contact with certain services and, therefore, are not represented in the literature. This is part of the problem in researching marginalized, "invisible" populations (Cordray & Pion, 1991). The literature shows that kids generally come from places where abuse occurred in one way or another, and that abuse is part of the life-story of these young people. But still I wondered if the reason few explanations exist as to why certain adolescents end up on the street and others do not is due to research constraints (i.e., the use of questionnaires or structured interviews which do not encourage a plethora of responses). In addition to learning that roughly 75 percent of females and 40 percent of males on the street have been abused in one form or another, I wanted to understand how those experiences shaped their lives, how those traumas led them to the street. What about those experiences is still reflected in the lives that they lead as street kids? Are they still engaged in abusive relationships? Are they in an abusive relationship with society? Are they the whipping people? Is this a metaphor that would resonate for them? Recent literature suggests that street kids relate to one another in ways that might have been modelled for them in the abusive relationships that they lived in at home (Hagan & McCarthy, 1997; Plympton, 1997) and that some of those patterns resemble unstable connections with others.

Life on the Street

Life on the street has been characterized in a number of different ways, often with descriptions of the overt characteristics of the street youth population. The literature has typically looked at specific behaviors (e.g., crime and delinquency, prostitution, substance abuse, etc.) to further describe what happens to youth when they become street kids. There are few accounts of the experiences of youth as they make the transition to the street other than what has previously been described by the typology set forth by Palenski and Launer (1987) and a few brief explications on the transition to the street (Lundy, 1995; Plympton, 1997). There are even fewer accounts of the psychosocial ramifications of that experience

(McCarthy & Hagan, 1992). Through reading the literature I noticed that there are four areas of behavior commonly associated with street life: (a) crime, delinquency, and prostitution; (b) substance abuse; (c) sexual behavior; and (d) suicide ideation and attempts.

Crime and Delinquency

Historically, street youth have been considered a threat to the "order" of society and have often been characterized as delinquent kids who don't care about the ideals held by the majority of society (Ek & Steelman, 1988). This view of street kids has become more widespread in recent years, positing that kids in general are folk devils (Schissel, 1997), and street kids, in particular, are dangerous criminals (Carlen, 1996; Shane, 1996). The view that street kids are already criminals when they get to the street is challenged by the proposition that crime, delinquency, and prostitution are effects of a criminogenic situation, as opposed to deficiencies or delinquent tendencies within the adolescents themselves (Hagan & McCarthy, 1997; McCarthy & Hagan, 1991). The representations of street kids fascinated me as I read about kids who engage in crime and prostitution. It is interesting (although I'm unsure about how or why it is interesting) that youth who engage in criminal behavior, even if it is petty theft, are rarely categorized as being resilient, malleable, adaptable to the lifeworld of the street (Carlen, 1996; McCarthy & Hagan, 1992). From one perspective, I understand that criminal behavior is not seen as a good coping strategy and is seen as a threat to the order of our society, but on the other hand, these kids do find a way to survive and perhaps the ability to do so needs to be understood in terms of positive survival skills (Hagan & McCarthy, 1997; Whitbeck & Simons, 1993). I lamented the fact that kids are too rarely seen as innovative, ingenious souls who, by hook or by crook, make their lives on the street despite the obstacles. The sequelae behavioral characteristics of youth living on the street often include engagement in criminal activities, although it has been suggested that this is not the preferred route for most street kids, but rather a necessity (Palenski, 1984, cited in McCarthy & Hagan, 1991).

The impetus for criminal behavior among street youth has been debated for years. The debate centers around whether or not youth living on the street have a priori delinquent characteristics before coming to the street, or whether or not it is the experience of the street that provides the structure in which criminal behavior is a viable solution (see Hagan & McCarthy, 1997, for a discussion on the ontogenic and sociogenic aspects of crime for street kids). The criminogenic hypothesis proposed by Hagan and McCarthy (1991) contends that youth engage in illegal activities as a result of the phenomenon of living on the street or being homeless. They conclude that as time spent on the street increases, so does criminal activity and severity of crimes committed. This was evidenced in a study conducted in Toronto, Canada, wherein all types of crime increased after more than 12 months were spent on the street (McCarthy & Hagan, 1991). Further to their study, Hagan and McCarthy (1997) expanded their vision of the criminogenic situation to include considerations of both the ontogenic and the sociogenic aspects which influence and impact street kids' criminal behaviors. But still, there are not a plethora of studies that explore youth poverty, lack of employment, safe, clean, affordable housing, and other contextual influences which would ultimately impact kids' lives on the street (for exceptions, see Carlen, 1996, Hagan & McCarthy, 1997; Ruddick, 1996; Shane, 1996).

There are a number of contributing components to the criminogenic situation on the street. Whitbeck and Simons (1993) contend that exposure to abuse while at home increases adolescents' anti-social adaptation strategies, and consequently these adolescents engage in deviant subsistence strategies to survive on the street. In addition, adolescents are at a particular disadvantage for engaging in legal employment as a result of their young age. McCarthy and Hagan (1991) suggest that economic stability is nearly impossible to achieve for adolescents, and that criminal behavior is one method for earning money.

Although Russell (1998) found that 44.2 percent of street kids had never been detained in jail or juvenile hall overnight, crime is, nevertheless, a major focus of the research on street kids. According to the research, the kinds of crimes committed by street youth vary. Typically street youth are classified into two categories: (a) status offender and (b) delinquent. Status crimes include running away, truancy, and disobedience, whereas delinquent offenses include those which would be considered felonious in the adult court system (United States). Delinquent offenders are further separated into violent and non-violent categories. In a study designed to assess whether or not maltreatment and specific kinds of maltreatment (i.e., sexual, physical, emotional, etc.) among youth would determine the type of court involvement (or the kinds of crimes committed), Famularo et al. (1990) reported that among 189 status offenders and an equal number of delinquent offenders, 52 percent and 42 percent, respectively, reported some kind of maltreatment at home. Of the status offenders, 74 percent identified as being runaways and 35 percent of those identified having been sexually abused. Statistical analyses illustrated that for status offenders, maltreatment distinguished runaways from non-runaways, and for delinquent offenders, physical abuse discriminated between violent and non-violent offenders (27 percent of violent offenders reported having been physically abused, as compared to 14 percent of non-violent delinquent offenders). What remains to be answered is what happens to adolescents' sense of identity and self when they engage in illegal activity? McCarthy and Hagan (1991, 1997) conclude that as time spent on the street increases, so, too, will criminal behavior, but I wonder why that is. Is that because choices diminish for youth living on the street for an extended period of time? Hagan and McCarthy (1997) would suggest that it is. Or is this connected to what Palenski and Launer (1987) refer to as the development of a "runner identity" and all that is entailed in that identity? The literature is quiet on what is behind the criminal behavior and how that behavior affects the esteem of youth on the street.

Prostitution

Theories abound that sexual abuse plays a significant role in discriminating between adolescents who will engage in prostitution and other criminal activity, and those who will not (McCormack et al., 1986). Research indicates that early sexual trauma or sexual abuse is correlated to prostitution (Radford et al. 1991; Seng, 1989; Simons & Whitbeck, 1991; Webber, 1991) and delinquency (Bowers, 1990), although no direct links have been established. There is some speculation that (a) running away is the middle step that connects sexual abuse to prostitution (Famularo et al.,

1990; Spatz Widom & Ames, 1994), or (b) that engagement in criminal behavior once on the street connects sexual abuse to prostitution through the criminogenic situation of being homeless (McCarthy & Hagan, 1991; Simons & Whitbeck, 1991). Whatever the case, prostitution or "survival sex" (sex in exchange for money, food, or shelter) is a behavior in which many street youth engage (Feitel et al., 1992; McCarthy & Hagan, 1991; Rotheram Borus, Bahlberg, Koopman, & Rosario, 1992; Russell, 1998; Terrell, 1993).

It is noteworthy that the literature which investigates prostitution does not discuss self and/or identity in the selling of the body. I haven't been able to find that kind of information, but it is the kind of information I would like. Participation in prostitution may be correlated to a myriad of factors once getting to the street (Hagan & McCarthy, 1997; Russell, 1998). This component of the phenomenon is not as well represented in the literature as I would have liked. Research concentration in the area of adolescent prostitution revolves around family background and sexual abuse. In 1985, a Canadian study of 42 child prostitutes in Vancouver found that 80 percent of the girls and 17 percent of the boys had been sexually abused at home, mostly by men. It is suggested that most prostitutes come from families that are sexually destructive, physically violent, or mentally cruel (Webber, 1991).

In a comparison study of adolescent and adult homeless females (Simons & Whitbeck, 1991), 33 percent of the runaways reported that sexual abuse was the causal factor for leaving home. In the same study, 18 percent of adolescent as compared to 11 percent of adult respondents had engaged in prostitution. Moreover, in regression analyses, child sexual abuse proved to be the only significant predictor for prostitution among the runaway population. Another kind of comparative study was undertaken to discriminate between adolescent prostitutes and sexually abused adolescents (Seng, 1989). Although the groups were similar to each other on variables such as demographic characteristics, family constitution, parental use of alcohol or drugs, domestic violence, truant behavior, poor grades, and psychological difficulties (including depression, suicidal ideation, and poor self-image), the factors that discriminated between the two groups included emotional conflict, parental neglect, physical abuse, and certain behavior characteristics, the most salient of which included (a) drug and alcohol use, (b) justice system contact, and (c) runaway episodes.

The findings related to prostitution do not bode well for adolescents who leave home for the street. Although these adolescents may be fleeing situations as bad or worse than what the street can provide, it seems that prostitution is a new kind of abuse, an abuse that is somehow sanctioned by a society that has a hand in structuring what street life is like for kids. Recently, prostitution among street youth has been re-defined to focus on prostitution as a form of child abuse (Children Involved in Prostitution, 1997).

Living on the street reconstructs to some degree the abusive relationships adolescents experienced at home (Plympton, 1997; Terrell, 1993). The reality of the street includes being hungry, lonely, scared, cold, and a willingness to do whatever it takes to survive. Webber (1991) claims that

> [t]hose who can't abide the abuse and who feel forced to flee run a great risk of being rescued by a pimp. Family life has prepared them to become a particular kind of victim in a particular subculture. Sex, they have learned, is a ticket to love; their sex is the only asset they have to offer. (100)

In effect, the literature describes the risk of prostitution once on the street, and the likelihood of coming from a particular kind of family. What this literature does not depict, describe, or divulge is the lived experience of "hooking." For example, if front-line workers want to aid in keeping young women from falling into the traps of a pimp, information about how pimps approach new street kids would be useful, not to mention understanding what it takes to negotiate your way out. Additionally, the literature does not answer questions about issues around selling oneself for the first time, the transition into prostitution, battery in prostitution relationships, involvement with the justice system, or knowing how to avoid the "heat scores" (areas where there are police or dangerous areas for being picked up by police). These types of data are not present in the literature on street kids and would be useful in explicating the experience of youth who make their way there. Do we know what a kid experiences when she is raped and beaten by her pimp? Do we know what the ramifications are of being pimped, sold, and bought by men who pretend to love you? Do we know about the difficulty prostitutes face when they want to get out? Are we clear about the sexual orientation issues that emerge (especially for men) as they prostitute themselves? Does the literature explain how developing dependencies on drugs or pimps or prostitution contributes to the structure of life on the street? Is there any talk about the role of drugs and addiction in pimp's domination of young prostitutes? Do we understand the sense of betrayal young prostitutes feel when they come to understand the parameters of a pimped relationship? Are we clear about how to help prostitutes break the seemingly narcotic nature of prostitution itself? Have we investigated how these women feel in a society that is largely patriarchal? Do we know what the men feel around issues of measuring up to a "male image," and consequently how they feel being outside of the mainstream? Do we know about how prostitutes feel when residential committees rally to get them out of their communities and what the psychological ramifications of being shunned are? And lastly, what happens to a street kid's sense of self when that sense of self is intermingled with the additional identity of "hooker?" These are some of the questions that arise as I think about the prostitutes that I knew in my work on the street. Who do these kids become? This is but another example of how separated the lived realities of the street are from the representations in the literature. These questions are not adequately dealt with in the literature, and again, this may be partly because in-depth studies encapsulating these kinds of questions (phenomenological, interpretive, hermeneutic, ethnographic, etc.) have not been undertaken nearly enough.

Substance Abuse

Substance abuse is an important issue confronting street youth for two reasons: (a) It is cited in the literature as a behavioral characteristic represented in the families from whence street children emerge, and (b) it is a behavioral characteristic which is prevalent among the street adolescents themselves (Bradley, 1997; Delacoste & Alexander, 1987; Fors & Rojek, 1991; Hagan & McCarthy, 1997; Radford et al., 1991; Ruddick, 1996, Russell, 1998, Warheit & Biafora, 1991; Webber, 1991). The general prevalence rates for substance abuse vary because operational definitions of substance abuse have not been, and are not consensually agreed upon

(McCarty, Angeriou, Heubner, & Lubran, 1991). Despite that fact, substance abuse has been found to be as high as 94 percent among a recent homeless youth sample (Russell, 1998).

Compared to similar groups of school children, adolescent runaways generally exhibit higher rates of substance use (Fors & Rojek, 1991). And, according to Hagan and McCarthy's (1997) hypothesis of street kids being influenced both by ontogenic and sociogenic circumstances, drug use and other illegal substance abuse patterns are likely to increase with time spent on the street. Radford et al. (1991) report that not all street youth engage in hard drug use (like cocaine or crack), and that the drugs most often used on the street are marijuana and psychedelics with prevalence rates of 85.6 percent, and 81.9 percent, respectively (Russell, 1998). Among prostitutes, statistics indicate that 68 percent of respondents report being users of drugs, alcohol, or both (Radford et al., 1991).

These data tweak my curiosity about what "using" on the street is like for street kids. There is some evidence to suggest that using is a social part of being on the street (Plympton, 1997). I wonder if one can stay clean on the street. Are kids enjoying their substance use? Do kids use to avoid the pain, fear, and exploitation they live on the street? Does using numb them? Does it transport them to a place where all is well? Is it "cool?" Are they addicted? Are they afraid of addiction? Do kids see substance use as a destructive behavior? Who benefits from the drug trade on the street? How is the street set up to maintain this kind of activity? These are some of the questions I wondered about after learning about the prevalence rates reported in the literature.

Substance abuse and HIV. With the advent of the human immunodeficiency virus (HIV) and its transmission routes (i.e., intravenous drug use [IVDU] and sharing of drug-related paraphernalia), substance abuse issues have most recently centered around the HIV risk associated with common substance abuse practices (Bradley, 1997). There is consensual agreement in the literature that IVDU poses a serious health threat (HIV and other blood-bound diseases) to homeless adolescents (Athey, 1991; Koopman, Rosario, & Rotheram Borus, 1994; Millstein, 1990; Radford et al., 1991; Rotheram Borus, Koopman, & Ehrhardt, 1991; Shane, 1996; Yates, MacKenzie, Pennbridge, & Cohen, 1988). The prevalence of IVDU among homeless adolescents ranges between 15 percent to 34 percent (Athey, 1991; Russell, 1998; Yates et al., 1988); however it has been reported as low as 0.3 percent in one study (Koopman et al., 1994). One explanation for the variance in prevalence rates is attributed to geographical location and the availability of injectable drugs. More alarming than the prevalence rates for IVDU among homeless kids is the prevalence of sharing drug paraphernalia (e.g., spoons, needles, cotton filters, water, etc.), which has been shown to be a transmission route for HIV. The sharing rate is reported to be roughly 33 percent (i.e., one or more occasions of sharing drug paraphernalia) for both males and females using injectable drugs (Rosenthal, Moore, & Buzwell, 1994). Here again, the literature does not investigate the relationship problems that arise for youth who do not want to share needles and paraphernalia. In my experience working with IV drug users, I learned that there is a code of behavior around using drugs, and that code reinforces comradeship among street kids who use. Questions like what the psychosocial consequences are for youth who refuse to engage in communal drug use or refuse to share paraphernalia are missing from the literature but probably do affect sharing and are of significant importance. Despite the absence from the literature, these issues are realities on the street and do correspond to a greater psychosocial issue for street kids, namely, that of relationships and the manifestations thereof among street friends. My questions are: Do kids realize the risk that they run by using? By sharing? If they do understand, what is at risk for them as they engage in high-risk behavior? Is it worth it to them to share anyway? Is that the price of belonging? Additionally, clarity around how kids cope with HIV from a psychological point of view is missing from the literature, since it is primarily concerned with the overt behavior of drug use and abuse.

Sexual Behavior

Little is known about the sexual behaviors of homeless adolescents (Forst, 1994). Prevalence rates on sexual activity among homeless youth have been reported as high as 92 percent (Greenblatt & Robertson, 1993). Given that statistic, it is astonishing to learn that as many as 30 percent of homeless youth report never using a condom (Koopman et al., 1994), and 30 percent of sexually active youth report having more than ten partners in the previous year (Greenblatt & Robertson, 1993).

Aside from these frightening statistics, there are real concerns about the HIV risk among the adolescent homeless population. Part of the problem is that youth may practice safe sex when working in the sex trade (Russell, 1998), but when it comes to their personal relationships, the concepts of safety and protection do not seem to apply (Athey, 1991). The issue becomes further complicated by sexual activity with IV drug users. In one study, 18 percent of respondents reported knowingly having sex with an IVDU (Greenblatt & Robertson, 1993). And lastly, unprotected sex, which seems to be frequent between friends and lovers on the street, leads to an astonishing rate of teenage pregnancy. Athey (1991) cites the prevalence rate for pregnancy at 31 percent among homeless women between the ages of sixteen and nineteen.

These data depict a lifestyle which, among other things, is hazardous to the adolescents' health. Between higher rates of substance abuse, and a strong correlation between frequent abuse of substances, and increased numbers of sexual partners (Koopman et al., 1994; Radford et al., 1991), coupled with unsafe sex practices (i.e., inconsistent or non-existent condom use), and IV drug use, homeless adolescents are at increased risk for both HIV and other sexually transmitted diseases. What is relevant to me, however, is the differential use of condoms in sexual behavior between friends and sexual behavior for work (or shelter, food, or drugs). For example, what I learned while working on the street is that this difference is particularly problematic for adolescent men, who identify themselves as heterosexual, engage in homosexual prostitution, and then engage in intercourse with their female friends without protection. Research studies that investigate sex, drugs, and any combination thereof have not conceived of the problems broadly enough to take in the multifarious problematics of life on the street.

There seems to be a lacuna in the literature regarding the pressure felt by youth on the street to behave in specific ways, and more broadly, how their particular sense of the future affects their decision-making processes around adhering to safer behaviors. Russell (1998) found that sexually transmitted disease risk increased with time on the street for young women, especially as they may be engaging in sexual risk-taking. She suggested that the increased risk correlated to the increased time perhaps as a result of pressure on the street to engage in either sex-work or to engage in sex on the street with peers. But despite these informative statistics, we do not know what the issues are beyond the tallying of overt behaviors represented in the literature.

Suicide

Suicide is a significant concern for the street youth population. Thirty percent to 37 percent of adolescent runaways report attempting suicide at least once, with 20 percent to 50 percent making more than one attempt (Rotheram Borus, 1993; Stiffman, 1989a). Over the past 25 years, the adolescent suicide rate in the general population has increased roughly 300 percent, culminating in an alarming rate of ten deaths for every 100,000 adolescents (Rotheram Borus, 1993). This statistic says nothing about how many attempted suicides there are. What still remains unclear, despite the statistics, is what makes street youth particularly vulnerable to suicidal acts and ideation. Rotheram Borus (1993) suggests that the stressful life of the street, coupled with youths' troubled backgrounds creates an atmosphere for depression and increased risk for suicide. Russell (1998) found that homeless youth who had spent days without food had attempted suicide 3.9 times more often than kids who had not spent days without food. As well, sexually abused youth seem to be at particular risk for suicide (Janus et al., 1987; Kurtz, Kurtz & Jarvis, 1991; McCormack et al., 1986; Rimsza et al., 1988), which suggests that the destructive families that produce runaways (throwaways etc.) may inadvertently kill them. Confirmatory evidence exists in that homeless adolescents cite difficulty at home as the most common precipitating factor leading to their suicide attempts (Rotheram Borus, 1993; Stiffman, 1989a). Moreover, 80 percent of the adolescents responding to a survey about suicide reported that they made the attempt the same day that they thought about killing themselves (Stiffman, 1989a). This is a troubling finding because the literature does not explain what particular events of that day made the adolescent decide that s/he would attempt/commit suicide. I wonder about whether or not the temporal layout of thinking and attempting suicide is different for adolescents on the street as compared to adolescents living at home. With the numbers as alarming as they are, perhaps some of the mitigating factors around life on the street and the particular incidents that led up to the suicide/attempt could be investigated to expose what seems to be a bit of a mystery in the literature (Rotheram Borus, 1993). And, as has been shown with respect to other issues confronting street youth, the literature does not seem to be broad enough, holistic enough, or deep enough to uncover the experiences youth face as they face themselves, society, and life on the street. What does their despair mean? Although Bradley (1997) begins to ask these questions, and reports that 16.9 percent of the sample reported feeling lonely, these measures are part of a depression scale and are not connected into the textures and complexities of life on the street for kids. Are street kids hopeless, helpless, lost, sad? These are the kinds of questions I think would open up the space in which kids' experiences could be understood.

Suicide and sexual orientation. Another significant issue around suicide on the street is the number of homeless gay and lesbian adolescents (Kruks, 1991). It is estimated that between 18 percent to 40 percent of homeless adolescents are gay or lesbian (Nelson, 1994; Russell, 1998). In addition to the stresses that all youth on the street share, homosexual youth face increased levels of stress as a result of their orientation; in fact sexual orientation is often cited as the precipitating factor for leaving home (Kruks, 1991). The suicide rate among gay and lesbian adolescents is roughly three times the average for heterosexual adolescents (Gentry & Eron, 1993, cited in Nelson, 1994), and of known adolescent suicides, 30 percent are identified as gay or lesbian. These findings seem to be consistent with the increased risk for suicide among sexually abused homeless adolescents. The risk of suicide among these youth (sexually abused and homosexual) seems to be exacerbated by their particular issues in addition to the stresses of street life, and is a serious concern for the well-being of kids on the street.

Considerations

It is clear that adolescents who flee or are kicked out of home face substantial obstacles and risks for healthy (physically and emotionally), functional lives. I have tried to provide information about the substantive components of the literature by (a) investigating whatever is known about the antecedents of wanting to leave home and the sequelae events around leaving the home, and (b) providing data about the overt characteristics of life on the street. Throughout I have attempted to demonstrate how the literature has contributed to what we know or understand about the realities of life on the street for adolescents, and conversely, what the literature has failed to explicate. I've tried to illustrate specifically where the literature is deficient in dealing with psychological, emotional, and/or social aspects of life on the street by posing questions throughout the text that the literature has raised for me. I believe that the gaps in the literature are staggering. Both from substantive as well as methodological points of view, these gaps nonetheless have served, in part, as the impetus for getting me to the street.

Many issues related to homeless adolescents are not represented in the literature or are minimally mentioned. Although the research has defined, described, and delineated between kinds of homeless adolescents, their familial circumstances, and their lives on the street, the literature has not provided a comprehensive picture of the experiences of these youngsters. For the most part, the literature is fragmented and compartmentalized. Issue by issue, researchers have dissected and investigated components of the phenomenon, leaving trails of the parts without any sense of the whole. In an effort to explicate certain aspects of the street, the literature has become de-humanized. I have attempted to explicate where de-humanization has occurred by deconstructing the literature in a search for what is and what is not present in it.

Part of the process of deciphering what is going on with homeless adolescents has led to a dichotomy between academic research and the circumstances of street life. There has been a focus on overt, behavioral, and measurable aspects of homelessness and somewhat of a disregard for the experiences therein, that is, the lived realities of youth have been reduced to prevalence rates. In recent efforts (e.g., Carlen, 1996; Lundy, 1995, Hagan & McCarthy, 1997), researchers have been approaching the topic in a more holistic manner and have been bringing to bear the complexities of this phenomenon. I am encouraged by some of the studies

I have seen and hope that a more ecological approach continues to evolve in connecting the lived experiences of street life to the academic discourses which take up these issues.

From my standpoint, there are certain issues which I would expect the literature to address. I have tried to interweave the unanswered questions into my text. Still there are other issues which are minimally represented in the literature and would be excellent sources of information in understanding street kids. These include: (a) issues around partner battery; (b) gender roles on the street (e.g., Pfeffer, 1997); (c) racism on the street, including the emergence and growing popularity of a strong Nazi youth movement (i.e., skinheads); (d) the role of patriarchy on the street and the pecking order among street kids; (e) the importance of friends on the street, including concepts of street families (e.g., Plympton, 1997); and (f) violence on the street, specifically around issues of fear. There are additional substantive issues which I think are missing from the literature.

The following group of gaps in the literature correspond to issues that frame the experience of being an adolescent on the street. These issues include: (a) understanding the transitions that adolescents make at a number of different stages in making the street their home including: (i) first arriving on the street, (ii) getting to know the ropes of the street, (iii) finding out about services, (iv) surviving the street, and (v) getting off the street; (b) understanding kids' perceptions about mainstream adults, and looking at the effects of those views on service delivery, and interventions; (c) looking at street life from the perspective of the postmodernist, as an alternative to mainstream, capitalist, urban life; and (d) investigating the interface between the phenomenon of being a street kid and the services that are set up to respond to the needs of this population, including service providers and policymakers. It would also be interesting to explore how youth on the street experience themselves as welfare recipients and drop-in attendees. How do kids interpret the discourses of the street? How do they make meaning of themselves, of society, and of street life? How does the world appear to street kids, and what role does the mainstream have in creating that vision?

Another interesting component of the literature which became apparent to me is the way in which youth have been characterized. According to the findings of the studies that investigate street youth, a composite depiction of a homeless adolescent might look as follows: a substance-abusing, prostituting, suicidal, sexually promiscuous (with little regard for health issues), criminal young person who has somehow failed and ended up on the street. There is an overwhelming body of research which depicts the unfortunate reality of homeless adolescents. This research objectifies street youth. It connotes that these youth are the undesirable "other;" they are the disenfranchised; they are the marginalized, the subculture from which mainstream society wants to distance itself. As previously mentioned, there is too little mentioned of survival skills, of resilience or coping mechanisms, or of anything framed in a positive way. There is similarly little mention of the social context in which issues like abuse and poverty arise and the ramifications thereof for street kids (for an exception, see Hagan & McCarthy, 1997). The focus is upon the adolescent on the street, separate and apart from the society that produces them and helps to structure their lives as "other."

From my perspective, this body of literature is located in the positivistic paradigm which assumes a singular view of reality and has utilized the "scientific" method for finding the answers. Consistent with that philosophy, it follows that the problematic nature of this body of research stems from the overwhelmingly singular approach to understanding street kids and their lives. I found that the vast majority of the studies which I reviewed utilized self-report/survey-type measures to facilitate descriptive and discriminant analyses with the goal of expounding on the issues related to adolescent homelessness (and the components thereof). Although the kinds of data that are gathered from these kinds of studies have provided me with the starting point for this study, I believe that there are intrinsic problems with self-report, survey-type studies. Like any questionnaire, these kinds of investigations do not have the facility to delve into the deeper meanings that street kids ascribe to their lives, nor do they capture the experienced realities of these kids from their points of view. I submit that because of the pervasive use of quantitative designs, a certain kind of knowledge has been put forward with respect to street kids. The result of this kind of research is that we're left with a specific kind of information. This is to say that although we may be able to *predict* that 75 percent of female street kids have been sexually abused, we know very little about who these people are, what their lives are like, what running to the street has given them, what stories they tell about themselves, about us, about their lives; and who they think they'll be in the future. More simply put, the literature that has been accumulated in the street kid domain has all but left out the protagonists themselves in the street scene.

I believe that there is sufficient information about what kinds of issues confront street youth (I am specifically referring to overt characteristics and behaviors exhibited by street kids and measurable/quantifiable by researchers). Quantitative research has described and defined youth at risk and youth on the street. This is evidenced by prevalence rates for drug use, sexual behavior, prostitution involvement, criminal behavior, and so on. Research must now explore the phenomenon as experienced by street kids. Information is needed to inform on how street kids make meaning of their lives. Understanding is critical to inform on the complexity of this phenomenon. From querying how youth structure their lives as well as probing how society structures street kids lives, issues of self and identity are certain to emerge. A synthesis of information between the academe and homeless adolescents must be undertaken to develop a comprehensive picture of the experience of living on the street. This may enable service providers to deliver what is needed, and would also enable academics to reconnect to the lived experiences of street kids.

Lastly, the paradigm in which homeless youth have traditionally been studied must include variety. The positivistic, reductionist model seems to be inadequate in presenting a broader sense of what happens to these kids on the street. In other words, the positivist model has its limitations as does any other kind of research approach. Since there has been little qualitative research done with street kids, I believe that an opportunity exists to approach the phenomenon from a wholly different perspective. To this end, I have tried to shift paradigmatic gears in exploring the streetscape in an effort to meet street kids where they are at, and to listen to the stories that they tell about their lives.

Appendix II

Figure 2   *T-Shirt: Front*

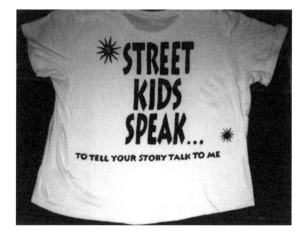

Figure 3   *T-Shirt: Back*

Appendix III

Figure 4   *Placard: Photo by T. Pirosok*

References

Adams, G. R., Gullotta, T., & Clancy, M. A. (1985). Homeless adolescents: A descriptive study of similarities and differences between runaways and throwaways. *Adolescence, 20*(79), 715–724.

Administrative Report. (1998). City of Vancouver: File No. 3504. *Standing Committee of Planning and the Environment* [on line]. Available: http://www.city.vancouver.bc.ca/ctyclerk/cclerk/980430/pe4.htm

Alexander, P. C. (1992). Application of attachment theory to the study of sexual abuse. *Journal of Consulting and Clinical Psychology, 60,* 185–195.

Athey, J. L. (1991). HIV infection and homeless adolescents. *Child Welfare, 70*(5), 517–528.

Baron, S. (1989). Resistance and its consequences: The street culture of punks. *Youth & Society, 21*(2), 207–237.

Becvar, R. J., & Becvar, D. S. (1994). The ecosystemic story: A story about stories. Special Issue: Couple and family therapy: A constructivist/ecosystemic view. *Journal of Mental Health Counseling, 16*(1), 22–32.

Bonneycastle, S. (1996). *In search of authority: An introductory guide to literary theory* (2nd ed.). Peterborough, ON: Broadview.

Bowers, L. B. (1990). Traumas precipitating female delinquency: Implications for assessment, practice and policy. *Child and Adolescent Social Work, 7*(5), 389–401.

Bowler, T. D. (1981). *General systems thinking: Its scope and applicability.* New York: North Holland.

Bradley, J. (1997). *Runaway youth: Stress, social support and adjustment.* New York: Garland.

Brannigan, A., & Caputo, T. (1993). *Studying runaways and street youth in Canada: Conceptual and research design issues*. (1993). User Report: Responding to Violence and Abuse. Ottawa, Canada: Solicitor General of Canada.

Breitbart, M. M. (1998). "Dana's mystical tunnel": Young people's design for survival and change in the city. In T. Skelton & G. Valentine (Eds.), *Cool places: Geographies of youth culture* (pp. 305–327). New York: Routledge.

Britzman, D. P. (1991). *Practice makes practice: A critical study of learning to teach*. Albany, NY: SUNY Press.

Bylaw 3M99. (1999). The City of Calgary.

Bylaw 6478. (1998). The Corporation of The City of New Westminster.

Bylaw 6555/95. (1995). The City of Winnipeg.

Bylaw 7885. (1998). City of Vancouver.

Capra, F. (1982). *The turning point: Science, society, and the rising culture*. New York: Bantam.

———. (1996). *The web of life: A new scientific understanding of living systems*. New York: Doubleday.

Caputo, J. D. (1987). *Radical hermeneutics: Repetition, deconstruction, and the hermeneutic project*. Bloomington: Indiana University Press.

Caputo, T., Weiler, R., & Kelly, K. (1994a). *Phase II of the runaway and street youth project: General introduction and overview*. (1994–10). User Report: Responding to Violence and Abuse. Ottawa, Canada: Solicitor General of Canada.

———. (1994b). *Phase II of the runaway and street youth project: The Ottawa case study*. (1994–11). User Report: Responding to Violence and Abuse. Ottawa, Canada: Solicitor General of Canada.

Carlen, P. (1996). *Jigsaw: A political criminology of youth homelessness*. Buckingham, UK: Open University Press.

Carlson, B. E. (1991). Outcomes of physical abuse and observation of marital violence among adolescents in placement. *Journal of Interpersonal Violence, 6*(4), 526–534.

Children Involved in Prostitution. (1997). *Report by the task force on children in prostitution*. Minister of Alberta Family and Social Services.

Cordray, D. S., & Pion, G. M. (1991). What's behind the numbers? Definitional issues in counting the homeless. *Housing Policy Debate, 2*(3), 587–616.

Colby, I. C. (1990). The throw-away teen. *The Journal of Applied Social Sciences, 14*(2), 277–294.

Community and Neighbourhood Services. (1998). Squeegee diversion strategy for street-involved homeless youth. *City Toronto* [on line]. Available: http://www.city.toronto.on.ca/legdocs/agendas/committees/cn/cn98100j/it001.htm

Cresswell, T. (1998). Night discourse: Producing/consuming meaning on the street. In N. R. Fyfe (Ed.), *Images of the street: Planning, identity and control in public spaces* (pp. 268–279). New York: Routledge.

Crouch, D. (1998). The street in the making of popular geographical knowledge. In N. R. Fyfe (Ed.), *Images of the street: Planning, identity and control in public spaces* (pp. 160–175). New York: Routledge.

Crowhurst, B., & Dobson, K. (1993). Informed consent: Legal issues and applications to clinical practice. *Canadian Psychology, 34*(3), 329–346.

Csapo, M. (1987). Running away from or running away to? *Canadian Journal of Special Education, 3*(1), 31–51.

Dadds, M. R., Braddock, D., Cuers, S., & Elliott, A. (1993). Personal and family distress and personal correlates. *Community Mental Health Journal, 29*(5), 413–422.

Daly, G. (1998). Homelessness and the street: Observations from Britain, Canada, and the United States. In N. R. Fyfe (Ed.), *Images of the street: Planning, identity and control in public spaces* (pp. 111–128). New York: Routledge.

Daly, H. E. (1996). *Beyond growth: The economics of sustainable development*. Boston: Beacon.

Delacoste, F., & Alexander, P. (Eds.). (1987). *Sex work: Writings by women in the sex industry*. Pittsburgh, PA: Cleis.

De Man, A., Dolan, D., Pelletier, R., & Reid, C. (1993). Adolescent runaways: Familial and personal correlates. *Social Behavior and Personality, 21*(2), 163–167.

———. (1994). Adolescent running away behavior: Active or passive avoidance? *Journal of Genetic Psychology, 155*(1), 59–64.

Denzin, N. (1997). *Interpretive ethnography: Ethnographic practices for the 21ˢᵗ century*. Thousand Oaks, CA: Sage.

Dewey, J. (1916). *Democracy and education*. New York: Macmillan.

Domestic Relations Act, Chapter D-37. Alberta: Canada (1980).

Earls, C. M. (1990). Early family and sexual experiences of male and female prostitutes. *Canada's Mental Health, December*, 7–11.

Ek, C. A., & Steelman, L. C. (1988). Becoming a runaway: From the accounts of youthful runners. *Youth and Society, 19*(3), 334–358.

Ellul, J. (1964). *The technological society*. New York: Vintage.

Famularo, R., Kinscherff, R., Fenton, T., & Bolduc, S. M. (1990). Child maltreatment histories among runaway and delinquent children. *Clinical Pediatrics, 29*(12), 713–718.

Feitel, B., Margetson, N., Chamas, J., & Lipman, C. (1992). Psychosocial background and behavioral and emotional disorders of homeless and runaway youth. *Hospital and Community Psychiatry, 43*(2), 155–159.

Fors, S. W., & Rojek, D. G. (1991). A comparison of drug involvement between runaways and school youths. *Journal of Drug Education, 21*(1), 13–25.

Forst, M. (1994). Sexual risk profiles of delinquent and homeless youths. *Journal of Community Health, 19*(2), 101–114.

Fox, D., & Prilleltensky, I. (Eds.). (1997). *Critical psychology: An introduction*. Thousand Oaks, CA: Sage.

Fyfe, N. R. (Ed.). (1998). *Images of the street: Planning, identity and control in public space*. New York: Routledge.

Gadamer, H. G. (1977). *Philosophical hermeneutics*. Berkeley: University of California Press.

———. (1995). *Truth and method*, 2nd (Rev. ed.). New York: Continuum.

———. (1997). Reflections on my philosophical journey. In L. E. Hahn (Ed.), *The philosophy of Hans-Georg Gadamer* (pp. 3–63). Chicago: Open Court Publishing.

Gallagher, S. (1992). *Hermeneutics and education*. Albany, NY: SUNY Press.

Gergen, K. J. (1994). *Realities and relationships: Soundings in social construction*. Cambridge, MA: Harvard University Press.

Gibson, S. (1998). Bosson's attack on panhandlers: Throw the beggars out. *C4LD MegaCouncil Watch Page* [on line]. Available: http://www. web.net/~citizens/megaw/begging.html

Giroux, H. (1996). *Fugitive cultures: Race, violence & youth.* New York: Routledge.

————. (1997). *Channel surfing: Race talk and the destruction of today's youth.* New York: St. Martin's.

————. (2000). *Stealing innocence: Youth, corporate power, and the politics of culture.* New York: St. Martin's.

Grant, G. (1995). *Philosophy on the mass age.* (Edited with an introduction by W. Christian). Toronto: University of Toronto Press.

Greenblatt, M., & Robertson, M. J. (1993). Life-styles, adaptive strategies, and sexual behaviors of homeless adolescents. *Hospital and Community Psychiatry, 44*(12), 1177–1180.

Guidano, V. F. (1995a). A constructivist outline of human knowing processes. In M. J. Mahoney (Ed.), *Cognitive and constructive psychotherapies: Theory, research, and practice* (pp. 89–102). New York: Springer.

————. (1995b). Constructivist psychotherapy: A theoretical framework. In R. A. Neimeyer & M. J. Mahoney (Eds.), *Constructivism in psychotherapy* (pp. 93–108). Washington: American Psychological Association.

Hagan, J., & McCarthy, B. (1997). *Mean streets: Youth crime and homelessness.* Cambridge, UK: Cambridge University Press.

Herbert, S. (1998). Policing contested space: On patrol at Smiley and Hauser. In N. R. Fyfe (Ed.), *Images of the street: Planning, identity and control in public spaces* (pp. 225–235). New York: Routledge.

Heschel, A. J. (1962). *The prophets.* New York: Harper & Row.

Hesson, K., Bakal, D., & Dobson, K. (1993). Legal and ethical issues concerning children's rights of consent. *Canadian Psychology, 34*(3), 317–328.

Hetherington, K. (1998). Vanloads of uproarious humanity: New age travellers and the utopics of the countryside. In T. Skelton & G. Valentine (Eds.), *Cool places: Geographies of youth culture* (pp. 328–342). New York: Routledge.

Hier, S. J., Korboot, P. J., & Schweitzer, R. D. (1990). Social adjustment and symptomatology in two types of homeless adolescents:

Runaways and throwaways. *Adolescence, 25*(100), 761–771.

Hurwitz, E., & Hurwitz, S. (1997). *Coping with homelessness.* New York: Rosen.

Ibáñez, T., & Íñiguez, L. (Eds.). (1997). *Critical social psychology.* Thousand Oaks, CA: Sage.

Jackman Cram, S., & Dobson, K. (1993). Confidentiality: Ethical and legal aspects for counselling. *Canadian Psychology, 34*(3), 349–363.

Janus, M. D., Archambault, F. X., Brown, S. W., & Welsh, L. A. (1995). Physical abuse in Canadian runaway adolescents. *Child Abuse and Neglect, 19*(4), 433–447.

Janus, M. D., Burgess, A. W., & McCormack, A. (1987). Histories of sexual abuse in adolescent male runaways. *Adolescence, 22*(86), 405–417.

Jardine, D. W. (1990). Awakening from Descartes' nightmare: On the love of ambiguity in phenomenological approaches to education. *Studies in Philosophy and Education, 10*, 211–232.

———. (1992). The fecundity of the individual case: Considerations of the pedagogic heart of interpretations. *Journal of Philosophy of Education, 26*, 51–61.

———. (1998). *To dwell with a boundless heart: Essays in curriculum theory, hermeneutics, and the ecological imagination.* New York: Peter Lang.

Jones, L. P. (1988). A typology of adolescent runaways. *Child and Adolescent Social Work Journal, 5*(1), 16–29.

Kashubeck, S., Pottebaum, S. M., & Read, N. O. (1994). Predicting elopement from residential treatment centers. *American Journal of Orthopsychiatry, 64*(1), 126–135.

Katz, C. (1998). Disintegrating developments: Global economic restructuring and the eroding of ecologies of youth. In T. Skelton & G. Valentine (Eds.), *Cool places: Geographies of youth culture* (pp. 130–144). New York: Routledge.

Koopman, C., Rosario, M., & Rotheram Borus, M. J. (1994). Alcohol and drug use and sexual behaviors placing runaways at risk for HIV infection. *Addictive Behaviors, 19*(1), 95–103.

Korten, D. C. (1998). *Globalizing civil society: Reclaiming our right to power.* New York: Seven Stories Press.

Kruks, G. (1991). Gay and lesbian homeless/street youth: Special issues and concerns. Special Issue: Homeless youth. *Journal of Adolescent Health, 12*(7), 515–518.

Kufeldt, K., Durieux, M., Nimmo, M., & McDonald, M. (1992). Providing shelter for street youth: Are we reaching those in need? VII International Congress on Child Abuse and Neglect (1988, Rio de Janeiro, Brazil). *Child Abuse and Neglect, 16*(2), 187–199.

Kufeldt, K., & Nimmo, M. (1987a). Youth on the street: Abuse and neglect in the eighties. Sixth International Congress: Child Abuse and Neglect (1986, Sydney, Australia). *Child Abuse and Neglect, 11*(4), 531–543.

————. (1987b). Kids on the street they have something to say: Survey of runaway and homeless youth. *Journal of Child Care, 3*(2), 53–61.

Kurtz, P. D., Jarvis, S. V., & Kurtz, G. L. (1991). Problems of homeless youths: Empirical findings and human services issues. *Social Work, 36*(4), 309–314.

Kurtz, P. D., Kurtz, G. L., & Jarvis, S. V. (1991). Problems of maltreated runaway youth. *Adolescence, 26*(103), 543–555.

Lee, D. (1998). *Body music*. Toronto, ON: Anansi.

Lees, L. (1998). Urban renaissance and the street: Spaces of control and contestation. In N. R. Fyfe (Ed.), *Images of the street: Planning, identity and control in public spaces* (pp. 236–253). New York: Routledge.

Loeb, R., Burke, T. A., & Boglarsky, C. A. (1986). A large-scale comparison of perspectives on parenting between teenage runaways and non-runaways. *Adolescence, 21*, 921–931.

Lopiano-Misdom, J., & De Luca, J. (1997). *Street trends: How today's alternative youth cultures are creating tomorrow's mainstream markets*. New York: Harper Collins.

Lundy, K. C. (1995). *Sidewalks talk: A naturalistic study of street kids*. New York: Garland.

Lyddon, W. J. (1995). Forms and facets of constructivist psychology. In R. A. Neimeyer & M. J. Mahoney (Eds.), *Constructivism in psychotherapy* (pp. 69–92). Washington: American Psychological Association.

Macdonald, C. (1999). Inaction opened kettle of fish. *Kingston Whig Standard*, July 30, p. 7.

Mahoney, M. J. (1988a). Constructive metatheory: l. Basic features and historical foundations. *International Journal of Personal Construct Psychology, 1*, 1–35.

————. (1988b). Constructive metatheory: ll. Implications for psychotherapy. *International Journal of Personal Construct Psychology, 1*, 299–315.

————. (Ed.). (1995). *Cognitive and constructive psychotherapies: Theory, research, and practice.* New York: Springer.

Marcuse, H. (1964). *One-dimensional man.* (Introduction by D. Kellner, 1991). Boston: Beacon.

Massey, D. (1998). The spacial construction of youth cultures. In T. Skelton & G. Valentine (Eds.), *Cool places: Geographies of youth culture* (pp. 121–129). New York: Routledge.

Mayers, M., & Olafson, L. (1997). From burning Barbie to living on the street: The consequences of political resistance among school aged girls. In A. Richardson (Ed.), *Childhood and youth: A universal odyssey* (pp. 268–279). Edmonton, AB: Kanata Learning Co.

McCarthy, B., & Hagan, J. (1991). Homelessness: A criminogenic situation? *British Journal of Criminology, 31*(4), 393–410.

————. (1992). Surviving on the street: The experiences of homeless youth. *Journal of Adolescent Research, 7*(4), 412–430.

McCarty, D., Angeriou, M., Huebner, R. B., & Lubran, B. (1991). Alcoholism, drug abuse, and the homeless. Special Issue: Homelessness. *American Psychologist, 46*(11), 1139–1148.

McCormack, A., Janus, M. D., & Burgess, A. W. (1986). Runaway youths and sexual victimization: Gender differences in an adolescent runaway population. *Child Abuse and Neglect, 10*(3), 387–395.

McWhirter, J. J., McWhirter, B. T., McWhirter, A. M., & McWhirter, E. H. (1994). High- and low-risk characteristics of youth: The five Cs of competency. *Elementary School Guidance and Counseling, 28*(3), 188–196.

Miller, A. T., Eggertson-Tacon, C., & Quigg, B. (1990). Patterns of runaway behavior within a larger systems context: The road to empowerment. *Adolescence, 25*(98), 271–289.

Millstein, S. G. (1990). Risk factors for AIDS among adolescents. *New Directions for Child Development, 50*(winter), 3–15.

Neimeyer, R. A., & Mahoney, M. J. (Eds.). (1995). *Constructivism in psychotherapy*. Washington: American Psychological Association.

Nelson, J. A. (1994). Comment of special issue on adolescence. *American Psychologist, 49*(6), 523–524.

Palenski, J. E., & Launer, H. M. (1987). The "process" of running away: A redefinition. *Adolescence, 22*(86), 347–362.

Pfeffer, R. (1997). *Surviving the street: Girls living on their own*. New York: Garland.

Pile, S., & Thrift, N. (1995). *Mapping the subject: Geographies of cultural transformation*. New York: Routledge.

Pipher, M. (1994). *Reviving Ophelia: Saving the selves of adolescent girls*. New York: Ballantine.

Plass, P., & Hotaling, G. T. (1995). The intergenerational transmission of running away: Childhood experiences of the parent of runaways. *Journal of Youth and Adolescence, 24*(3), 335–348.

Plympton, T. J. (1997). *Homeless youth creating their own "street families."* New York: Garland.

Powers, J. L., Eckenrode, J., & Jaklitsch, B. (1990). Maltreatment among runaway and homeless youth. *Child Abuse and Neglect, 14*(1), 87–98.

Powers, J. L., & Jaklitsch, B. (1993). Reaching the hard to reach: Educating homeless adolescents in urban settings. *Education and Urban Settings, 25*(4), 394–409.

Prilleltensky, I. (1994). *The morals and politics of psychology: Psychological discourse and the status quo*. Albany, NY: SUNY Press.

Radford, J. L., King, A., & Warren, W. K. (1991). *Street youth and AIDS*. Kingston, ON: Queen's University Press.

Ricoeur, P. (1981). Hermeneutics and the human sciences. In J. B. Thompson (Ed. and Trans.). *Paul Ricoeur—Hermeneutics and the human sciences: Essays on language, action and interpretation* (pp. 145–164). London: Cambridge University Press.

Rimsza, M. E., Berg, R. A., & Locke, C. (1988). Sexual abuse: Somatic and emotional reactions. *Child Abuse and Neglect, 12*(2), 201–208.

Risser, J. (1997). *Hermeneutics and the voice of the other: Re-reading Gadamer's philosophical hermeneutics*. Albany, NY: SUNY Press.

Rosenthal, D., Moore, S., & Buzwell, S. (1994). Homeless youths: Sexual and drug-related behaviour, sexual beliefs and HIV/AIDS risk. *AIDS Care, 6*(1), 83–94.

Roszak, T., Gomes, M. E., & Kanner, A. D. (Eds.). (1995). *Ecopsychology: Restoring the earth—healing the mind.* San Francisco, CA: The Sierra Club.

Rotheram Borus, M. J. (1993). Suicidal behavior and risk factors among runaway youths. *American Journal of Psychiatry, 150*(1), 103–107.

Rotheram Borus, M. J., Bahlburg, H. F., Koopman, C., & Rosario, M. (1992). Lifetime sexual behaviors among runaway males and females. *Journal of Sex Research, 29*(1), 15–29.

Rotheram Borus, M. J., Koopman, C., & Ehrhardt, A. A. (1991). Homeless youths and HIV infection. Special Issue: Homelessness. *American Psychologist, 46*(11), 1188–1197.

Ruddick, S. (1996). *Young and homeless in Hollywood: Mapping social identities.* New York: Routledge.

———. (1998). Modernism and resistance. In T. Skelton & G. Valentine (Eds.), *Cool places: Geographies of youth culture* (pp. 343–360). New York: Routledge.

Russell, L. (1998). *Child maltreatment and psychological distress among urban homeless youth.* New York: Garland.

Schissel, B. (1997). *Blaming children: Youth crime, moral panics and the politics of hate.* Halifax, NS: Fernwood.

Schweitzer, R. D., & Hier, S. J. (1993). Psychological maladjustment among homeless adolescents. *Australian and New Zealand Journal of Psychiatry, 27*(2), 275–280.

Schweitzer, R. D., Hier, S. J., & Terry, D. (1994). Parental bonding, family systems, and environmental predictors of adolescent homelessness. *Journal of Emotional and Behavioral Disorders, 2*(1), 39–45.

Seng, M. J. (1989). Child sexual abuse and adolescent prostitution: A comparative analysis. *Adolescence, 24*(95), 665–675.

Shane, P. G. (1996). *What about America's homeless children? Hide and seek.* Thousand Oaks, CA: Sage.

Simons, R. L., & Whitbeck, L. B. (1991) Sexual abuse as a precursor to prostitution and victimization among adolescent and adult homeless women. *Journal of Family Issues, 12*(3), 361–379.

Sixel, F. W. (1988). *Crisis and critique: On the 'logic' of late capitalism.* New York: Brill.

Smith, D. (1994). *Pedagon: Meditations on pedagogy and culture.* Bragg Creek, AB: Makyo.

Smith, N. (1996). *The new urban frontier: Gentrification and the revanchist city.* New York: Routledge.

Spatz Widom, C., & Ames, M. A. (1994). Criminal consequences of childhood sexual victimization. *Child Abuse and Neglect, 18*, 303–317.

Stefanidis, N., Pennbridge, J., MacKenzie, M. D., & Pottharst, K. (1992). Runaway and homeless youth: The effects of attachment history on stabilization. *American Journal of Orthopsychiatry, 62*(3), 442–446.

Stiffman, A. R. (1989a). Suicide attempts in runaway youths. *Suicide and Life Threatening Behavior, 19*(2), 147–159.

———. (1989b). Physical and sexual abuse in runaway youths. *Child Abuse and Neglect, 13*(3), 417–426.

Sullivan, E. (1990). *Critical psychology and pedagogy: Interpretation of the personal world.* Toronto, ON: OISE Press.

Terrell, N. E. (1993). *The violent world of homeless and runaway adolescents: An investigation of severe risk factors among homeless and runaway adolescents.* Unpublished doctoral dissertation, Iowa State University, Iowa.

University of Calgary, Research policy, Ethics of human studies (1996). *University of Calgary.* Calgary: Alberta.

Valentine, G., Skelton, T., & Chambers, D. (1998). Cool places: An introduction to youth and youth culture. In T. Skelton & G. Valentine (Eds.), *Cool places: Geographies of youth culture* (pp. 1–32). New York: Routledge.

Van der Ploeg, J. D. (1989). Homelessness: A multidimensional problem. Special Issue: Runaway, homeless, and shut-out children and youth in Canada, Europe, and the United States. *Children and Youth Services Review, 11*(1), 45–56.

Van Manen, M. (1991). *Researching lived experience: Human science for an action sensitive pedagogy.* London, ON: The University of Western Ontario Press.

Violato, C., & Travis, L. (1994). *Advances in adolescent psychology.* Calgary, AB: Detselig Enterprises.

Warheit, G. J., & Biafora, F. (1991). Mental health and substance abuse patterns among a sample of homeless post-adolescents. *International Journal of Adolescence and Youth, 3*(1–2), 9–27.

Warren, J. K., Gary, F., & Moorehead, J. (1994). Self-reported experiences of physical and sexual abuse among runaway youths. *Perspectives in Psychiatric Care, 30*(1), 23–28.

Webber, M. (1991). *Street kids: The tragedy of Canada's runaways.* Toronto: University of Toronto Press.

Whitbeck, L. B., & Simons, R. L. (1990). Life on the streets: The victimization of runaway and homeless adolescents. *Youth and Society, 22*(1), 108–125.

————. (1993). A comparison of adaptive strategies and patterns of victimization among homeless adolescents and adults. *Violence and Victims, 8*(2), 135–152.

Yates, G. L., MacKenzie, R. G., Pennbridge, J., & Cohen, E. (1988). A risk profile comparison of runaway and non-runaway youth. *American Journal of Public Health, 78*(7), 820–821.

Zide, M. R., & Cherry, A. L. (1992). A typology of runaway youths: An empirically based definition. *Child and Adolescent Social Work Journal, 9*(2), 155–168.